FINGER-TIP CHINESE

FINGER-TIP CHINESE

GET TO KNOW THE REAL CHINA

by Walter Long

with Liu Keming

New York · WEATHERHILL · Tokyo

First edition, 1996

Published by Weatherhill, Inc.
568 Broadway, Suite 705
New York, N.Y. 10012

Printed in the U.S.A.

Library of Congress
Cataloging in Publication Data

Long, Walter
    Fingertip Chinese : get to know the real China /
    by Walter Long — 1st ed.
        p.   cm.
    ISBN 0–8348–0362–3 (soft)
    1. Chinese language — Conversation and
    phrase books — English
I. Title
PL1125.E6L66   1996   96–4411
495.1'83421 — dc20   CIP

96 97 98 99 10 9 8 7 6 5 4 3 2 1

Contents

Introduction

About You

This book is for you if you are planning to visit China and are determined not to let the language barrier prevent you from enjoying yourself as you would in a country whose language you understand. A curious and adventurous traveler, you are accustomed to interacting with the local people you encounter, but you lack the time or opportunity to study Chinese intensively in preparation for your trip.

You need some help. But you do not wish to plough through grammatical explanations or memorize cumbersome expressions; you do not want a primer in the Chinese language disguised as a phrasebook. You want a brief and organized list of serviceable words and expressions, a list comprehensible both to yourself and to your Chinese hosts. And you want some background information on etiquette and customs—not an encyclopedic survey of Chinese culture, but brief pointers on what to say and do to put both you and your hosts at ease in typical situations. Providing such a tool is the goal of *Fingertip Chinese*.

About Phrasebooks

Most Chinese phrasebooks seem written by people who either never had to actually use them or perhaps, having spent many years studying the language, have a perverse interest in making communicating with the Chinese seem difficult. Favoring long-winded and elevated expression over the commonsense approach dictated by the situation, they advise us to inquire: *Qǐng wèn, nǐ néng tuījiàn yíwèi hǎo yákē dàifu ma?* (Can you recommend a good dentist?), when *Yákē dàifu zài nǎr?* (Where's a dentist?) is both more easily uttered and more readily understood. Moreover, if you need to see a dentist in China, it is likely an emergency; you should simply head straight for the nearest luxury tourist hotel and inquire in English.

Phrasebooks are also typically padded with expressions that have limited utility for the ordinary visitor to China; a Berlitz guide teaches us: *Diàoyú xūyào zhēng dé xúkě ma?* (Do I need a permit to fish?). This is perfectly correct, but if you're on your own in China you want to travel light and there's no need to lug a lot of marginally useful stuff like this around.

About *Fingertip Chinese*

The purpose of this book is to help you communicate, not foist you off as an accomplished speaker of Chinese. The sentences and expressions given are simple and straightforward. Moreover:

Fingertip Chinese is task-oriented, that is, the words and phrases presented are those you will need to get something or get something done, whether a good price for a souvenir or a cold beer at a restaurant (rather than the warm one that would ordinarily be served). These tasks are grouped according to situations or places where they would most likely occur, which are listed as page headings. Only active vocabulary is presented for the most part; as long as your request is being understood or acted upon, you do not really need to understand the Chinese verbal response.

The text is also fully bilingual, with expressions clearly presented in both romanized form, so that you can verbalize them, and in Chinese characters, so that they can be read by a Chinese assisting you. If you encounter difficulty in making yourself understood, simply use your fingertip and point to the Chinese text for your request. Far from appearing odd, your action will provide a welcome tool that will help your hosts to understand and assist you.

Each of the seven chapters in this book introduces a main topic (traveling, shopping, eating, etc.), under which are grouped related tasks that visitors to China may need to accomplish, especially when traveling on their own (getting directions, finding and buying maps, ordering the best noodles). The first chapter is an exception in that it introduces general expressions (for times, dates, amounts) useful in many situations.

The expressions recommended for accomplishing each task are the most readily understood and simplest possible. If the expression will require modification for a particular situation, appropriate substitutions are listed below it, with the portion to be substituted indicated in bold in the original sentence. Page numbers in parentheses refer to extended lists of substitutions. For example:

> I want to buy **three.**
> *Wǒ xiǎngmǎi **sānge.*** (Numbers, p. 22)
> 我想买三个.

On page 22, you will find the vocabulary to change "three" to "one" or "two," etc.

In addition to useful words and expressions, *Fingertip Chinese* contains abundant "how-to" information for getting along on your own in China. Even if you do not attempt a single Chinese utterance, reading the introduction to each chapter and section, as well as the "Fingertips" at the end of each chapter, will make your time spent in China much more enjoyable.

About the Chinese Language

The term "Chinese" only imprecisely describes the family of dialects (Cantonese, Shanghaiese, etc.) spoken over the vast expanse of China, which differ so markedly from each other that they may be considered separate languages. The Chinese have moved to minimize the communication difficulties these regional dialects pose by establishing the standard Beijing dialect as a national language, which is now referred to as *Pǔtōnghùa*, (literally, the "Common Language"), and known in the West as Mandarin. In spite of the fact that many Chinese do not speak it as a first language, and many speak it with a regional accent, Mandarin is the most widely *understood* language in China (and in fact, used by more people, over a billion, than any other language in the world).

It is this language that is referred to here as Chinese, and although this book is intended more for those who do *not* plan to study the language in depth, a few general remarks about it are in order, due to its reputation as formidably difficult. It is true that Chinese is a tonal language, requiring some mastery of its tonal variations (four are used in Mandarin) in order to be clearly understood; the Chinese language also contains a number of important sounds that are not common in English. Moreover, the ideograms, the "characters" used to transcribe the language, can be complex and are myriad, with a knowledge of three thousand or so required for a moderate level of literacy.

However, these difficulties are mitigated by several factors. The grammatical structure of Chinese is extremely simple. Although the typical subject-verb-object word order ("I eat noodles") approximates English and other Romance languages, Chinese is not inflected for case and number; that is, the verb (in this case, *chī*, for "eat") remains the same in the Chinese equivalents of "I ate noodles," "We ate noodles," "I will eat noodles," etc. Furthermore, there are no articles (a, an, the), and no masculine, feminine, or even plural forms of nouns. These features enable one to acquire vocabulary at a fast pace, and readily integrate new words into basic structures to create variations of expression.

The complex written language, moreover, is

now transcribed in an officially adopted romanization system called *pinyin*. This is the system used in *Fingertip Chinese* and it is through this system that we will review Chinese pronunciation. However, one should not get the idea that *pinyin* is simply an artificial tool concocted so that non-Chinese can use the language while avoiding the "real" orthography; it is rather a true alternate form of the written language of China. *Pinyin* is used in street and shop signs around the country, as well as in schools to teach Chinese children their language. Therefore it is useful to study and learn in its own right.

About Chinese Pronunciation

As indicated earlier, Chinese have long been accustomed to working with the regional dialects that developed over the vast areas of their empire over thousands of years. Thus, unlike the Japanese, they are accustomed to hearing their language spoken badly, and are able to make sense in many cases even of a novice speaker's odd pronunciation. Furthermore, tones are *not* as critical as typical language and guidebooks frighten people into believing; common colloquial expressions such as *Nǐ hǎo ma?* ("How are you?") can be voiced with utterly flat intonation and will never be misunderstood.

However, since tones are an important component of the language and will help convey meaning when used correctly, they should be understood and practiced. Mandarin Chinese has four tones, indicated with a mark over the vowel of the syllable: a high, level tone (marked *ā*); a rising tone (*á*); a tone that falls then rises (*ǎ*); and a falling tone (*à*). These are also referred to as the "first tone" (high level), "second tone" (rising), "third tone" (falling and rising), and "fourth tone" (falling). As musical notation, they might appear something like the following:

first   second   third   fourth

The English language also has tonal modulation, of course, although it is actually sentence intonation and not a component of the vocabulary itself, as in Chinese. Still, it might be useful to think of the high, level tone voiced as the flat notes of the first line of the chorus of *Jingle Bells* ("jin-gle bells, jin-gle bells"), and the rising tone approximating that of the "yeah?" in "Oh, yeah?" (as when following the accusation "You're an idiot!"). The falling and rising tone follows a pattern similar to an exaggerated "uh-huh" (make it go down and up, as Goofy would say it), while the falling tone sounds like the "Hey!" you might exclaim at someone who pokes you in the ribs with his umbrella as he forces his way out of crowded elevator. One important feature of Mandarin tones to note is that when one third tone appears after another, the first third tone often changes to a second tone. Do not be unduly concerned with this rule, for the change happens naturally; try saying *Nǐ hǎo ma?* several times, and you will see that it is much easier to say "hello" as the Chinese do: *Ní hǎo ma?* Another important feature to note is that many short words, often grammatical markers such as *ma* in the expression above, do not carry tones.

Vowels in Chinese all have fairly precise English equivalents. As transcribed in *pinyin,* they correspond to the portions of the English words indicated in bold:

pinyin	English
a	as "f**a**ther"
ai	as "b**uy**"
ao	as "h**ow**"
e	as "b**u**sh"
ei	as "h**ay**"
i	as in "s**ee**," but as "h**er**" after *zh, ch, sh* and *r,* and as "p**u**t" after *z, c,* and *s*
ia	as in "**ya**wn"
iao	as in "m**eow**"
ie	as in "**ye**n"
o	as in "c**aw**"
ou	as in "l**ow**"
u	as in "wh**o**"
ü	as the German umlaut ü (purse your lips and say "ee")
ui	as in "w**ei**gh"
uo	as in "**wa**r"

Consonants call for a bit more attention, as several *pinyin* letters are unlike their English equivalents and correspond to sounds that are not particularly common in English.

c	as in "ca**ts**"
h	gutturally, as in the German "i**ch**"
g	always hard, as in "**g**et"
j	as in "**j**eer," with tongue close to the teeth
zh	as in "**j**ewel," with tongue further back
q	as in "**ch**eap," with tongue close to the teeth
ch	as in "**ch**ew," with the tongue farther back
r	as in the growl "g-**r-r**," with a buzz
z	as in "ki**ds**," with a buzz
x	between "**s**ee" and "**sh**e" ("**s**ee" with a lisp)

About Traveling in China

China is changing with exponential rapidity. After centuries of slumbering Sinocentric complacency, the nation threw off both Imperial and imperialist masters only to lurch headlong into a five-decade experiment with Marxism that wastefully diverted its powers. Now "China is back," as they say, and devouring everything modern in pragmatic Chinese fashion, with philosophy subordinated to economics. How it will turn out is anybody's guess, and any person or text claiming to know with certainty should be regarded with suspicion. The China you visit this year is not as described in the guidebooks of last year, and a trip a few years hence will reveal yet another China. (As an apt Buddhist saying has it, "You can't put your foot in the same stream twice.") China can be by turns fascinating and frightening, exhilarating and depressing, drab and stunningly colorful, exasperating and immensely rewarding. It has always been, and remains, a dream destination for the romantic traveler.

Chinese tourist services, on the other hand, do not enjoy a particularly shining reputation; visitors tend come to China in spite of rather than because of them. Often cited as the culprit here is a socialist economy that offers little incentive for the individual to excel, yet until recently has presented no threat of dismissal for poor job performance. It is also true that in much of China the material resources and infrastructure needed to support top-flight facilities are simply unavailable, and a corrupt and inept bureaucracy is not the best vehicle for ensuring that limited resources are rationally or fairly allocated. Whatever the reasons, the inevitable complaints of tourists who feel they are not getting their money's worth are typically met with surliness on the part of the Chinese, who feel that their foreign guests are simply too rich and too spoiled.

Thus anyone contemplating travel to China on a package tour should do so only if satisfied that the adventure itself will be worth it, and should dismiss the idea getting value for money in the realm of hotels, meals, and services. The truth is simply that the greater part of the price paid to CITS (China International Travel Service) by your travel agent is simply a hard-currency donation to the national coffers; only a modest amount will be expended on the local vendors who will support your trip, and very little will filter down to the man or woman in the street. If you have more money than time, however, a package tour is the only way to go, for it is the only way to get around the country with a modicum of comfort and efficiency.

On the other hand, those with plenty of time but limited means need not pay CITS a dime; these days, intrepid travelers who wish can go to China on their own. Visas are readily available from many consular offices; sometimes the presentation of round-trip plane tickets is required, sometimes not. There is never a hassle in Hong Kong, still the favored entry point, with cheap and prompt visa service, and discount air fares there available on many international carriers.

Experienced travelers, of course, know that the bored government service workers and surly bureaucrats they encounter along beaten tourist routes are not representative of the Chinese people; moreover they know that through a little effort—strolling through streets and alleys away from tourist areas, dropping into local restaurants for a snack, expressing interest in people and their work—they will sooner or later experience the rewarding and memorable personal encounters that make exotic travel worthwhile. And in doing so the truly curious, warm, and gregarious nature of the Chinese will be revealed. There is crime in China, of course, but tourists are typically victims only of petty theft such as pickpocketing, never crimes of violence. You can pretty much go where you want and do what you want in safety.

Fingertip Chinese, of course, is not a guidebook; for really getting out and around on your own in China, I would recommend a guide slanted toward the individual traveler, such as one of the Lonely Planet series (see "A Traveler's Library for China" on p. 194). However, I will reiterate that policies of the Chinese government (such as areas proscribed for travel), the stranglehold on tourism of CITS, and the vested interests of package-tour operators, have in the past joined forces with the natural obstacle of the language barrier to make getting out on your own in China seem impossible. These barriers are simply not insurmountable, and I hope that *Fingertip Chinese* can contribute toward eliminating at least one of them.

Getting Started

To interact at all with the Chinese *in* Chinese, you will need the expressions in this chapter. Basically, they are of two types: the greetings and responses required for daily use; and the "nuts and bolts" terms you will need to specify types, quantities, times, days, dates, and amounts. These latter appear in list form and will be referred to frequently. The following constitute perhaps the minimum list of expressions that all visitors to China should be armed with.

Hello! *Ní hǎo!* 你好！
Pronounced "knee how," this is actually a question (literally "You fine?") called out as a greeting at any time of the day. The simplest response is to repeat the greeting.

Good morning! *Zǎo!* 早！
Only in the morning is a specific greeting used in China; at other times of the day *Ní hǎo!* is fine. "Good evening," or *Wǎnān* is an expression of parting, as the English "Goodnight."

Goodbye. *Zàijìan.* 再见.
To this all-purpose parting expression can be added *Míngtiān jiàn* or "See you tomorrow." To those parting on a journey, special expressions such as *Yílù píngān* ("May your road be peaceful") or *Yílù shùn fēng* ("Favorable winds all the way"] may be used.

Pardon me. *Qǐng wèn.* 请问.
This expression (literally "May I ask?") is used to preface a question, e.g., *Qǐng wèn, xiànzài jídiǎn zhōng?* ("Excuse me, what time is it?"). If you are truly putting someone out, *Máfan níle* ("Sorry to trouble you") is useful.

I'm sorry. *Duìbuqǐ.* 对不起.
Although this may be used as *Qǐng wèn* above, it also serves as a true apology for some act or omission, and can be made more polite by prefacing it with *zhēn* ("really"): *Zhēn duìbuqǐ* ("I'm really sorry").

Thanks. *Xièxiè.* 谢谢.
This expression is as all-purpose as its English equivalent, and no one will take offense at your likely tendency to overuse it. The Chinese to whom it is addressed will likely respond with: *Méi shénma* ("It's nothing"); or *Bú xiè* ("No [need for] thanks"); or *Bú yào kèqi* ("Don't be polite").

That's not correct. *Bú duì.* 不对.
This is useful for getting started in disputing hotel bills or getting an itinerary corrected. Its opposite is *Duìle!* ("Right!").

Don't want it! *Bú yaò!* 不要!
Stated matter-of-factly and followed by *Xièxiè*, constitutes a polite refusal ("No, thanks") for anything you may be offered. Its exclamatory form may be used to drive away overly persistent peddlers.

Where is the toilet? *Cèsuǒ zài nǎr?* 厕所在哪儿?
It is useful also to learn the character for the Chinese toilet [厕所], which is sometimes indicated by the character for "Men" [男] or "Women" [女].

Tips on using some of the expressions below are given on pp. 18–19. In general, Chinese use "Please" and "Thank you" less often than do Westerners, but these expressions are still perfectly appropriate.

Hello!
Nǐ hǎo!
你好!

Good morning!
Zǎo!
早!

Goodbye.
Zàijiàn.
再见.

See you tomorrow.
Míngtiān jiàn
明天见.

Just a second.
Děng yīxìa.
等一下.

Pardon me.   (As in "May I ask?")
Qǐng wèn.
请问.

Sorry to trouble you.   (Requesting a favor)
Máfan nǐle.
麻烦你了.

I'm sorry.   (Apology for act or omission)
Dùibuqǐ.
对不起.

Remaining calm and polite is also your best bet for getting around the dreaded *Méi yǒu* (literally, "Isn't any," whether postage stamps, hotel rooms, etc.), which seems the Chinese service worker's knee-jerk response to any request.

Good.
Hǎo.
好.

Thanks.
Xièxie.
谢谢.

It's nothing.
Méi shénma.
没什么.

Not at all.
Bú xiè.
不谢.

It doesn't matter.
Méi yǒu guānxi.
没有关系.

Forget it.
Suànle.
算了.

No, thanks!   (As in "I don't want it!")
Bú yào!
不要!

Where is the toilet?
Cèsuǒ zài nǎr?
厕所在哪儿?

Chinese numbers are decimally based and follow a regular pattern of progression. Note that Chinese are familiar with Arabic numbers and use them often. Remember that the "i" in *shi* here is pronounced like the "er" in h**er**. After you master the words for one through ten it is easy to construct the higher-order numbers: "twenty-five," for example, is *èrshíwǔ*, literally "two tens and a five."

0	*líng*	零
1	*yī*	一
2	*èr*	二
3	*sān*	三
4	*sì*	四
5	*wǔ*	五
6	*liù*	六
7	*qī*	七
8	*bā*	八
9	*jiǔ*	九
10	*shí*	十
11	*shíyī*	十一
12	*shíèr*	十二
13	*shísān*	十三
14	*shísì*	十四
15	*shíwǔ*	十五
16	*shíliù*	十六
17	*shíqī*	十七
18	*shíbā*	十八
19	*shíjiǔ*	十九
20	*èrshí*	二十
21	*èrshíyī*	二十一
22	*èrshíèr*	二十二

"One hundred and sixty-four" would be *yìbǎi liùshísì*, literally "one hundred, six tens, and four." One exception to the regular pattern is *èr*, the number "two," which is prounced *liǎng* in combination with "hundreds" and higher multiples. Note that there is special term for "ten thousand" that is combined to make higher numbers, but you will likely have little need of these.

30	*sānshí*	三十
40	*sìshí*	四十
50	*wǔshí*	五十
60	*liùshí*	六十
70	*qīshí*	七十
80	*bāshí*	八十
90	*jiǔshí*	九十
100	*yìbǎi*	一百
101	*yìbǎilíngyī*	一百零一
102	*yìbǎilíngèr*	一百零二
123	*yìbǎi èrshísān*	一百二十三
130	*yìbǎi sānshí*	一百三十
1,000	*yìqiān*	一千
1,234	*yìqiān liángbǎi sānshísì*	一千两百三十四
2,000	*liǎngqiān*	两千
3,000	*sānqiān*	三千
5,000	*wǔqiān*	五千
10,000	*yíwàn*	一万
10,300	*yíwàn sānbǎi*	一万三百
100,000	*shíwàn*	十万
1,000,000	*yìbǎiwàn*	一百万

The following expressions are useful for describing quantities and amounts. For monetary amounts, see p. 28. Add *bèi* to numbers to make multiples.

How many?	*Duōshǎo?*	多少?
How much?	*Duōshǎo?*	多少?
How much money?	*Duōshǎo qián?*	多少钱?
How far?	*Duō yuǎn?*	多远?
How long (in time)?	*Duō jiǔ?*	多久?
How much longer?	*Hái yǒu duō jiǔ?*	还有多久?

about	*zuǒyòu*	左右
none	*méi yǒu*	没
enough	*gòule*	够了
almost	*chàbuduō*	差不多
just right	*gānggāng hǎo*	刚刚好
a few	*shǎo*	少
too few	*tài shǎo*	太少
a lot	*hěn duō*	很多
a little	*yìdiǎn*	一点
too much	*tài duō*	太多
too much (money)	*tài guì*	太贵
a pair	*yìshuāng*	一双
one dozen	*yìdá*	一打

double	*liǎngbèi*	两倍
triple	*sānbèi*	三倍
quadruple	*sìbèi*	四倍

The expression *fēnzhī* relates two numbers to form a fraction; *sānfēnzhīyī*, or "one third," is literally "of three parts, one." The word *dì* placed before a number creates an ordinal number, while *cì* placed after a number indicates number of "times."

one tenth	*shífēnzhīyī*	十分之一
one quarter	*sìfēnzhīyī*	四分之一
one third	*sānfēnzhīyī*	三分之一
three eighths	*bāfēnzhīsān*	八分之三
half	*yíbàn*	一半
five eighths	*bāfēnzhīwǔ*	八分之五
three quarters	*sìfēnzhīsān*	四分之三
nine tenths	*shífēnzhījiǔ*	十分之九

ten percent	*bǎifēnzhīshí*	百分之十
twenty percent	*bǎifēnzhīèrshí*	百分之二十
fifty percent	*bǎifēnzhīwǔshí*	百分之五十

first	*dìyī*	第一
second	*dìèr*	第二
third	*dìsān*	第三
fourth	*dìsì*	第四
tenth	*dìshí*	第十
hundredth	*dìbǎi*	第百

once	*yícì*	一次
twice	*liǎngcì*	二次
three times	*sāncì*	三次
four times	*sìcì*	四次
five times	*wǔcì*	五次
ten times	*shícì*	十次

Although China officially subscribes to the metric system, English units and a few of the traditional measurements still in use are included below.

It is **one centimeter** long.
*Zhè yǒu **yìgōngfèn** cháng.*
这有一公分长.

inch	*yīngcùn*	英寸
Chinese inch (3.3 cm)	*cùn*	寸
meter	*gōngchǐ*	公尺
foot	*yīngchǐ*	英尺
Chinese foot (.33 cm)	*chǐ*	尺
kilometer	*gōnglǐ*	公里
mile	*yīnglǐ*	英里
Chinese mile (.5 km)	*lǐ*	里

It weighs **one gram.**
*Zhè yǒu **yíkè** zhòng.*
这有一克重.

kilogram	*gōngjīn*	公斤
pound	*bàng*	磅
catty (.5 kg)	*jīn*	斤

It holds **one liter.**
*Zhè kéyǐ zhuāng **yìgōngshēng**.*
这可以装一公升.

quart	*kuātuō*	夸脱
Chinese quart (.8 l)	*shēng*	升
Chinese peck (10 l)	*dǒu*	斗

As other Asian languages, Chinese uses "counters," or "measure words" that follow numbers to enumerate different types of objects. Three pieces of paper, for example, would be counted *sānzhāng*, while three cups of tea would be counted *sānbēi*. In fact, however, using counters is not all that critical; in most cases, the general counter *gè*, can be used and will be understd. Note that the number "two" is prounced *liǎng*, rather than *èr*, in combination with counters.

most objects	*gè*	个
one glass	*yìge bēizi*	一个杯子
thin, flat objects	*zhāng*	张
three tickets	*sānzhāng piào*	三张票
establishments	*jiā*	家
two restaurants	*liǎngjiā cāntīng*	两家餐厅
long, thin objects	*píng*	瓶
four bottles of beer	*sìpíng píjiǔ*	四瓶啤酒
animals	*zhī*	只
five birds	*wǔzhī niǎo*	五只鸟
people	*wèi*	位
six doctors	*liùwèi dàifu*	六位大夫
vehicles	*liàng*	位
seven bikes	*qīliàng zìxíngchē*	七辆自行车
luggage	*jiàn*	件
eight pieces of luggage	*bájiàn xíngli*	八件行李

The item you will be certainly interested in counting is money, *qián*, for which the measure word is *kuài*, literally a "piece" or *yúan*, a "dollar". One-tenth of a dollar is a *jiǎo*, but is called *máo* when used to express a monetary amount; "cents" in Chinese are *fēn*. Note that these smaller denominations all have paper notes as well as coins.

¥ 740	*qībǎi sìshí kuài*	七百四十块（元）
	(or *qībǎi sìshí yuán*)	
¥ 500	*wúbǎi kuài*	五百块
¥ 320	*sānbǎi èrshí kuài*	三百二十块
¥ 300	*sānbǎi kuài*	三百块
¥ 100	*yìbǎi kuài*	一百块
¥ 74	*qīshísì kuài*	七十四块
¥ 50	*wǔshí kuài*	五十块
¥ 20	*èrshí kuài*	二十块
¥ 10.80	*shíkuài bāmáo*	十块八毛
¥ 9.50	*jiǔkuài wǔmáo*	九块五毛
¥ 5.00	*wǔkuài*	五块
¥ 3.00	*sānkuài*	三块
¥ 1.00	*yíkuài*	一块
¥ .75	*qīmáo wǔfēn*	七毛五分
¥ .63	*liùmáo sānfēn*	六毛三分
¥ .15	*yìmáo wǔfēn*	一毛五分
¥ .10	*yìmáo*	一毛
¥ .04	*sìfēn*	四分
¥ .03	*sānfēn*	三分
¥ .01	*yìfēn*	一分

These basic expressions should help you get where
you're going, or find your hotel if you're lost.

Go straight ahead.
Wǎng qián zǒu.
往前走.

Turn left.
Zuó zhuǎn.
左转.

Turn right.
Yòu zhuǎn.
右转.

It's **in the back.**
Zài hòumiàn.
在后面.

in front	*qiánmiàn*	前面
on the left	*zuǒmiàn*	左面
on the right	*yòumiàn*	右面
over there	*zài nàr*	在哪儿
upstairs	*lóushàng*	楼上
downstairs	*lóuxià*	楼下

Which way is **north?**
Nǎmiàn shì běi?
哪面是北?

south	*nán*	南
east	*dōng*	东
west	*xī*	西

After "How much?" and "Where?" the questions "When?" and "How long?" and the time expressions used to respond to them should prove most useful during your travels in China.

When?	*Shénme shíhòu?*	什么时候?
What time?	*Shénme shíjiān?*	什么时间?
What day?	*Nǎtiān?*	哪天?
What year?	*Nǎnián*	哪年?
How long?	*Duōjiǔ?*	多久?

It will take **half an hour.**
Xūyào bànge zhōngtóu.
需要半个钟头.

about an hour   *yíge zhōngtóu zuǒyòu*
一个钟头左右

more than three hours   *sāngè duō zhōngtóu*
三个多钟头

less than an hour   *búdào yígè zhōngtóu*
不到一个钟头

It opens at ten a.m.
Shàngwǔ shídiǎn kāimén.
上午十点开门.

It closes at six p.m.
Xiàwǔ liùdiǎn guānmén.
下午六点关门.

It's open from 10:00 to 6:00.
Shídiǎn kāimén, liùdiǎn guānmén.
午十点开门, 六点关门.

Note that Monday functions as the day dividing one week from the next in time expressions; "this Tuesday" refers to the Tuesday of this week, even if it fell three days ago; likewise, if today is Tuesday, "next Sunday" is not the Sunday of this coming weekend, but the Sunday after that.

We went **yesterday.**
Wǒmén zuótiān qùde.
我门昨天去的.

this morning	*jīntiān zǎochén*	今天早晨
this afternoon	*jīntiān xiàwǔ*	今天下午
the day before yesterday	*qiántiān*	前天
last Tuesday	*shàng Zhōuèr*	上周二
last week	*shàng zhōu*	上周
last month	*shàngge yuè*	上个月
last year	*qùnián*	去年

We begin **today.**
Wǒmén jīntiān kāishǐ.
我门今天开始.

immediately	*mǎshàng*	马上
right now	*xiànzài*	现在
in two hours	*liǎngge zhōngtóu yǐhòu*	两个钟头 以后
tomorrow	*míngtiān*	明天
the day after tomorrow	*hòutiān*	后天
next Monday	*xià Zhōuyī*	下周一
next week	*xià zhōu*	下周
next month	*xiàge yuè*	下个月
next year	*míngnián*	明年

Chinese days of the week follow a regular pattern, with the numbers one through six affixed to *xīngqī*, "week." The exception is Sunday, *Xīngqītiān*.

What day is today?
Jīntiān xīngqījǐ?
今天星期几？

Yesterday was Monday.
Zúotiān shì Xīngqīyī.
昨天是星期一．

Today is Tuesday.
Jīntiān shì Xīngqīèr.
今天星期二．

Tomorrow is Wednesday.
Míngtiān shì Xīngqīsān.
明天是星期三．

Will you be free on Thursday?
Xīngqīsì ní yǒu kòngma?
星期四你有空吗？

Friday is a holiday.
Xīngqīwǔ shì jiérì.
星期五是节日．

Let's meet on Saturday.
Wǒmén Xīngqīliù jiàn.
我们星期六见．

We're leaving on Sunday.
Wǒmén Xīngqītiān zǒu.
我们星期天走．

Months of the year are likewise very regular, with the numbers one through twelve preceding *yuè*, for "month."

What month is best?
Shénme yuè shí zuìhǎode ma?
什么月是最好的吗?

I can't bear Shanghai in August.
Wǒ shòubùliǎo Bāyuède Shànghǎi.
我受不了八月的上海.

I plan to spend October in Beijing.
Wǒ jìhuà Shíyuè zài Běijīng dùguò.
我计划十月在北京渡过.

The weather is great in **May.**
Wǔyuè de tiānqì zuìhǎo.
五月的天气最好.

January	*Yīyuè*	一月
February	*Èryuè*	二月
March	*Sānyuè*	三月
April	*Sìyuè*	四月
May	*Wǔyuè*	五月
June	*Liùyuè*	六月
July	*Qīyuè*	七月
August	*Bāyuè*	八月
September	*Jiǔyuè*	九月
October	*Shíyuè*	十月
November	*Shíyīyuè*	十一月
December	*Shíèryuè*	十二月

Time throughout China is set to Beijing time, and expressed officially according to a 24-hour clock. Conversationally, hours are expressed by affixing the numbers 1 through 12 (p. 22) to *diǎn zhōng* (literally, "point of the clock"), with *zhōng* often omitted. As usual, *liǎng* is used in place of *èr* for "two."

What time is it?
Xiànzài jídiǎn zhōng?
现在几点钟?

It's 1:00.
Yīdiǎn *zhōng.*
一点钟.

2:00	*liángdiǎn*	两点
3:00	*sāndiǎn*	三点
4:00	*sìdiǎn*	四点
5:00	*wúdiǎn*	五点
6:00	*liùdiǎn*	六点
7:00	*qīdiǎn*	七点
8:00	*bādiǎn*	八点
9:00	*jiúdiǎn*	九点
10:00	*shídiǎn*	十点
11:00	*shíyīdiǎn*	十一点
12:00	*shíèrdiǎn*	十二点

Expressions for minutes are also very regular, with *fēn*, for "minute," added to the numbers 1 through 60 (p. 22). Note the expressions added to clarify the period of the day: *zǎoshàng* for the morning; *xiàwǔ* for the afternoon, till 6:00 p.m.; *wǎnshàng* for the evening. Note that *fēn* is sometimes omitted.

The meeting is at **3:20 p.m.**
*Huìyì xiàwǔ **sāndiǎn èrshí** kāishǐ.*
会议下午三点二十开始.

The flight leaves at **8:03 a.m.**
*Fēijī zǎoshàng **bādiǎn língsānfēn** qǐfēi.*
飞机早上八点零三分起飞.

3:00	*sāndiǎn zhōng*	三点钟
9:05	*jiǔdiǎn língwǔ*	九点零五
10:10	*shídiǎn shífēn*	十点十分
11:15	*shíyīdiǎn shíwǔfēn*	十一点十五分
	(or *shíyīdiǎn yíkè*)	（十一点一刻）
12:20	*shíèrdiǎn èrshí*	十二点二十
1:25	*yìdiǎn èrshíwǔ*	一点二十五
2:30	*liángdiǎn sānshífēn*	两点三十分
	(or *liángdiǎn bàn*)	（两点半）
3:35	*sāndiǎn sānshíwǔ*	三点三十五
4:40	*sìdiǎn sìshífēn*	四点四十分
5:45	*wǔdiǎn sìshíwǔ fēn*	五点四十五分
6:50	*liùdiǎn wǔshífēn*	六点五十分
7:55	*qīdiǎn wǔshíwǔ fēn*	七点五十五分
noon	*zhōngwǔ*	中午
midnight	*yèbàn (wǔyè)*	夜半（午夜）

To express a date in Chinese, add *hào* to the number of the day, and *nián* to the number of the year. When stringing time expressions together, Chinese always start with the largest unit first: thus July 4, 1776 is *yīqiān qībǎi qīshíliùnián, Qīyuè, sìhào.*

What's the date today?
Jīntiān jǐhào?
今天几号？

Today is the twenty-fifth.
Jīntiān èrshíwǔhào.
今天二十五号.

We're arriving June seventeenth.
Wǒmén Liùyuè shíqīhào dào.
我门六月十七号到.

We're leaving on the twenty-first.
Wǒmén èrshíyī hào chūfā.
我门二十一号出发.

I first came to China in 1990.
Wǒ dìyícì lái Zhōngguó shìzài yījiǔjiǔlíngnián.
我第一次来中国是在一九九零年.

The People's Republic was founded on
    October 1, 1949.
*Zhōnghuá Rénmín Gònghéguó zài yījiǔsìjiǔnián
    Shíyuè yīhào chénglì.*
中华人民共和国在一九四九年
    十月一号　成立.

It is fun to watch the festivities of a Chinese holiday. Note that the dates listed in parentheses for the traditional holidays, the lower group below, refer to lunar months. You will have to inquire when they fall in any particular year.

Labor Day (5/1) is a national holiday.
Láodòngjié shì guójiā jiérì.
劳动节是国家节日.

New Year's Day (1/1)	*Yúandàn* (or Xīnián)	元旦 （新年）
Children's Day (6/1)	*Értóngjié*	儿童节
National Day (10/1)	*Gúoqìng*	国庆

When is the Dragon Boat Festival this year?
Jīnnián Dūanwǔjié shì jǐhào?
今年端午节是几号?

My favorite holiday is the **Spring Festival.**
Wǒ zuì xǐhuānde jiérì shì Chūnjié.
我最喜欢的节日是春节.

Lantern Festival (1/15)	*Yúanxiāojié*	元宵节
Pure Brightness Festival (4/5)	*Qīngmíngjié*	清明节
Dragon Boat Festival (5/5)	*Dūanwǔjié*	端午节
Mid-Autumn Festival (8/15)	*Zhōngqiūjié*	中秋节

Hints For Grammar Haters

Although it is a goal of *Fingertip Chinese* to avoid grammatical explanations, there are few basic patterns in Chinese that allow one to substitute newly learned vocabulary to create an unlimited number of expressions. Moreover, as mentioned previously, Chinese grammar is fairly simple. The typical subject-verb-object word order ("I eat noodles") approximates that of English, and it is not inflected for case and number, so that a verb, once learned, can be used in the same form regardless of tense and subject. Furthermore, there are no articles (a, an, the), and no masculine, feminine, or even plural forms of nouns. These features make it easy to create new expressions by substituting new vocabulary into basic structures.

Pronouns

It is handy to know the basic pronouns, so you don't have to repeat specific names or objects. The pronouns are:

wǒ	I	我
nǐ	you	你
tā	he, she, it	他, 她, 它

Adding the suffix *men* makes these plural:

wǒmen	we	我们
nǐmen	you	你们
tāmen	they	他们

Possessives

Adding the particle *de* creates simple possessives:

wǒde	my	我的
nǐde	your	你的
tāde	his, her, its	他的, 她的, 它的
wǒmende	our	我们的
nǐmende	your	你们的
tāmende	their	他们的

Nouns

Since nouns are not inflected for number, only context or a specific number will tell you exactly how many are being discussed. *Tāde shū* could mean "his book" or "his books" (or "her book" or "her books" for that matter).

The Equational Verb

This handy verb, "is," *shi* in Chinese, is useful for linking subjects with some information about them:

Wǒ shì Měigúorén.
I am an American.
我是美国人.

Zhèi shì wǒde.
This is mine.
这是我的.

Nà shì tāde.
That is hers.
那是她的.

Stative Verbs

These function more like English adjectives. A more extensive list of useful stative verbs appears on pp. 94–95. The most common and useful intensifier (specifically, an adverb) is *hěn* or "very."

> *Wó hǎo.*
> I'm fine.
> 我好.

> *Nà hén hǎo.*
> That's very good.
> 那很好.

> *Nèiběn shū hěn gùi.*
> That book is very expensive.
> 那本书很贵.

> *Nèiběn shū hén hǎo.*
> That book is very good.
> 那本书很好.

The pronunciation *hén* in the second and last sentences reminds us that when two third tone words appear in a row, the first changes to a second tone.

Transitive Verbs

Transitive verbs are those that take objects. Four of the most important for the visitor to China are:

> I'd like to **buy** a map.
> *Wǒ xiǎng**mǎi** dìtú.*
> 我想买地图.

> I'd like to **eat** fried rice.
> *Wǒ xiǎng**chī** chǎofàn.*
> 我想吃炒饭.

I'd like to **go** to Shanghai.
Wó xiǎngqù Shànghǎi.
我想去上海.

I'd like to **take** the train.
Wó xiǎngzuò huǒchē.
我想坐火车.

Negation

All three types of verbs (transitive, intransitive, equational) can be negated by placing "not" or *bu* before the verb.

Wǒ bú shì Měigúorén.
I'm not an American.
我不是美国人.

Nèiběn shū bù hǎo.
That book isn't good.
那本书不好.

Wǒ bú qù Shànghǎi.
I'm not going to Shanghai.
我不去上海.

An exception is the negation of existence, the chief verb for which is *yǒu* ("there exists," meaning "there is" or "there are"). This is negated by preceding it with *méi*; thus *méi yǒu* means "there isn't" or "there aren't." Since the availability of things (hotel rooms, train tickets, the food you want to eat) will have vital bearing on your daily routine in China, these are expressions you should memorize.

Questions

Questions are typically formed using one of two patterns. The first is the simple addition of *ma*, the question particle.

Nèiběn shū hǎoma?
Is that book good?
那本书好吗?

The second method is by combining both positive and negative verb forms, as we do in English when we ask "Are you going or not?" In Chinese:

Nǐ qù bu qù?
你去不去?

Nèiběn shū hǎo bu hǎo?
那本书好不好?

To reply, simply choose the verb form applicable:

Wǒ qù.
I'm going.
我去.

Wǒ bu qù.
I'm not going.
我不去.

Hǎo.
Yes, it's good.
好.

Bù hǎo.
No, it's not good.
不好.

Tense Particles

Chinese indicate past action by adding particles to the verbs, the most common of which are *guo*, indicating past experience, and *le*, indicating completed action. Choosing between them is sometimes tricky; pay attention to how the Chinese use them in their questions:

Have you ever been to Shanghai?
Shànghǎi nǐ qùguo méi yǒu?
上海你去过没有?

(Yes) I've been.
Qùguo.
去过.

Have you eaten?
Nǐ chīle méi yǒu?
你吃了没有?

(Yes) I've eaten.
Chīle.
吃了.

The train is here (i.e., has arrived).
Huǒchē láile.
火车来了.

Getting Settled

Next to getting tickets for travel between Chinese cities, finding suitable accommodations is probably the biggest headache for the individual tourist and the biggest drain on the resources of the budget-minded traveler. The reasons are threefold. First is the assumption on the part of all Chinese that you must stay in one of the grand hotels operated specifically for foreign tourists; in fact, in the past this was the law and officials of the Public Security Bureau (PSB, equivalent to a national police) generally enforced it. Although enforcement is much laxer now, whether you can stay in an establishment for Chinese travelers is very much up to the local PSB. Second is the problem of travel services in China in general; most are sorely overtaxed, and as a non-Chinese-speaking foreigner seeking a bargain by living among the locals, you are probably more trouble than your trade is worth. Finally, poor service is the rule with most government-run tourist facilities; those whose responsibility it is to cater to your needs for the most part have no incentive to do it well.

The bright exceptions here are joint-venture hotels, where workers are discovering the advantages (such as tips!) of providing good service, and local organizations that have discovered there is money to be made from catering to the needs of the individual budget traveler. Although the former are quite expensive, the latter are often reasonable and tend to be conveniently clumped together with cheap restaurants displaying English-language menus, bicycle rentals, etc. In Guangzhou, these can be found on Shamian Island, around the White Swan Hotel. In Beijing, try south of Liulichang (street of antique shops) and west of Tiantan (Temple of Heaven) Park. For specific recommendations, consult the latest edition of a good guide for individual travelers (Lonely Planet's *China* is recommended). If they are interested in you as a customer, touts outside of station areas can be useful; before deciding, make sure you get all the information about any lodgings offered, including the fee for taking you there and their location on your map. If things don't work out, you won't be getting a ride back.

Essential Expressions

Where's a hotel?
Bīnguǎn zài nǎr?
宾馆在哪儿?
Both *bīnguǎn* and *fàndiàn* are used to indicate hotels with services suitable for foreign visitors. This is a useful structure to practice in any event, as various sought-after items can be substituted (*Cèsuǒ zài nǎr?* Where's a toilet?). This expression leaves it up to the person questioned to figure out what type of establishment you might be seeking, however; if budget is a major consideration, try the following.

Where's an inexpensive hotel?
Piányìde fàndiàn zài nǎr?
便宜的饭店在哪儿？
This is probably a better way of getting the level
of accommodations you want than asking for the
location of a *lǚguǎn,* the inn that most traveling
Chinese would seek. Other low-level accommodations, called *lǚshè* and *zhāodàisuǒ,* are generally
not allowed to take foreigners in; however, if you
are solicited by a tout at a train station, you may
wish to check them out. The rule of thumb is
that if they allow you to stay, it is probably all
right with the local PSB.

I'd like to stay in a dorm room.
Wǒ xiǎng zhù sùshè.
我想住宿舍
Dormitory rooms will often be available at the
older Russian-built hotels (but not the newer
joint-venture hotels or international chains).

Do you have an empty room?
Kōngfángzi yǒu méi yǒu?
空房子有没有？
With luck, this will be met with an affirmative
response. More often, however, it will be met with
méi yǒu ("don't have"), a mantra of Chinese service workers that foreign visitors quickly learn to
loathe. However, don't be immediately discour-
aged and don't get angry; in fact, how well you
deal with this statement, and how many times

you successfully circumvent it, is a good barometer of how much you will enjoy your stay in China.

What should I do?
Zěnme bàn?
怎么办?
This is one of a number of phrases you might use to deal with the *méi yǒu;* it may solicit a suggestion for another place to try. Use the phrases on p. 50 to ask for other types of rooms; stress that you'll take anything. Say you'll sit in the lobby till something turns up; then have a seat and make good on your statement. Politeness and persistence generally pay off.

Arrive armed with adequate, bilingual city maps and an idea of where you want to go. Head for the bus stop if you don't want to spend money on a taxi, and don't be reluctant to ask for a ride from luggage-van drivers.

I'd like to go **here**.   (Showing map or address)
Wó xiǎngqù zhàr.
我想去这儿.

into town	*dào shìlǐ*	到市里
to the center of the city	*dào shìzhōng xīn*	到市中心

Can you take me here?
Nǐ bá wǒ dàidào zhàr, hǎomā?
你把我带到这儿, 好吗?

How much will it cost?
Duōshǎo qián?
多少钱?

Is there a cheaper way?
Yǒu méi yǒu piányídiǎnde?
有没有便宜点的?

Can I get there by bus?
Nàr tōng bù tōng qìchē?
那儿通不通车?

Where is the bus stop?
Qìchēzhàn zài nǎr?
汽车站在哪儿?

How much is the bus?
Zuò qìchē yào duōshǎo qián?
坐汽车要多少钱?

Good guide books are often your most reliable source for this information, at least for larger cities, where more options are available. Many small towns and cities have only one place where foreigners can stay.

Can you recommend a good hotel?
Qǐng gěi wǒ tuījiàn yíge fàndiàn, hǎoma?
请给我推荐一个好饭店, 好吗?

Can you recommend an inexpensive hotel?
Qǐng gěi wǒ tuījiàn yíge piányìde bīnguǎn, hǎoma?
请给我推荐一个便宜的宾馆, 好吗?

I'd like a hotel **near here.**
*Wǒ xiǎng **zài fùjìn** zhǎo jiā fàndiàn.*
我想在附近找家饭店

near the center of town	*shìzhōngxīn fùjìn* 市中心附近
near the airport	*fēijīchǎng fùjìn* 飞机场附近

Please write down the name and address.
Qǐng bǎ míngzi, dìzhǐ xiěxiàlái.
请把名子, 地址写下来.

Is it far? How far is it?
Yuǎn bù yuǎn? Duō yuǎn?
远不远? 多远?

Can I walk there?
Zǒuzhe qù yuǎn ma?
走着去远吗?

If you have no reservation, remember that patience and perseverance will pay off, as will a willingness to take anything offered.

I have a reservation. / I don't have a reservation.
Wǒ yǒu yùyuē. / *Wǒ méi yǒu yùyuē.*
我有预约. / 我没有预约.

I'd like a single room.
Wǒ xiǎngyào jiān dānfáng.
我想要间单房.

I'd like a double room.
Wǒ xiǎngyào jiān shuāngrénfáng.
我想要间双人房.

I want a room with a **bathroom.**
*Wǒ yào yìjiān dài **xǐzǎojiān** de kèfáng.*
我要一间带洗澡间的客房.

a fan	*diànshàn*	电扇
a TV	*diànshì*	电视
heating	*nuǎnqì*	暖气
air conditioning	*kōngtiáo*	空调

I'd like a place in the dorm.
Wǒ xiǎng zài xuéshēng sùshè zhǎo jiān fáng.
我想在学生宿舍找间房.

I'll take a bed anywhere.
Géi wǒ yìzhāng chuáng, zài nǎr dōu xíng.
给我一张床, 在那儿都行.

I'll sit here until someone checks out, OK?
Wǒ zuò zhàr děngdào yǒurén fùkuǎn líkāi, hǎoma?
我坐这儿等到有人付款离开好吗?

Individual travelers are still sometimes required to leave their passports at the desk, either as a security deposit or for review by PSB officials.

Can I see the room?
Wǒ kànkàn fáng hǎoma?
我看看房好吗?

How much is it?
Duōshǎo qián?
多少钱?

It's too **expensive.**
Tài **guì** le.
太贵了.

cold	*lěng*	冷
hot	*rè*	热
dark	*hēi*	黑
dirty	*zāng*	脏
noisy	*chǎo*	吵

Do you have anything **cheaper?**
*Yǒu méi yǒu zài **piányīdiǎnde?***
有没有再便宜点儿的?

larger	*dà yìdiǎnde*	大一点的
quieter	*ānjìng yìdiǎnde*	安静一点的
else	*biéde*	别的

I plan to stay **one** night.   (Numbers, p. 22)
*Wǒ dǎsuàn zhù **yíyè**.*
我打算住一夜.

I'm checking out.
Wǒ zhǔnbèi fùkuǎn líkāi.
我准备付款离开.

Chinese hotels (as opposed to the joint-venture luxury hotels) have a service counter *(fúwùtái)* at the center of each floor, offering laundry services, hot water for tea, fresh linens and towels, etc. Some hotels require that your room keys be left here while you are out.

Please give me my room key.
Qǐng bǎ wǒ fángjiān yàoshi géi wǒ.
请把我房间钥匙给我.

I need **hot water.**
Wǒ xūyào rèshuǐ.
我需要热水.

drinking water (cold boiled)	*liáng bǎi kāi*	凉白开
clean sheets	*gānjìng chuángdān*	干净床单
clean towels	*gānjìng máojín*	干净毛巾
a pillow	*zhěntóu*	枕头
a blanket	*máotǎn*	毛毯
toilet paper	*shóuzhǐ*	手纸
glasses	*bēizi*	杯子
tea cups	*chábēi*	茶杯
tea	*chá*	茶
soap	*féizào*	肥皂
shampoo	*xǐfàjì*	洗发剂
a toothbrush	*yáshuā*	牙刷
toothpaste	*yágāo*	牙膏
hangars	*yījià*	衣架

There is no tipping in China, although a "gratuity" for some special service requested, paid in advance, will often ensure that it gets done properly.

Please have the room cleaned.
Qǐng qīnglǐ fángjiān.
请清理房间.

I need these clothes washed.
Zhèxiē yīfu xūyào xǐ.
这些衣服需要洗.

When can I pick them up?
Wǒ shénme shíhòu lái qǔ?
我什么时候来取?

Where's the bathroom?
Cèsuǒ zài nǎr?
厕所在那儿?

Is there hot water all day?
Quántiān dōu yǒu rèshuǐ ma?
全天都有热水吗?

What time is the hot water on?
Shénme shíjiān shàng rèshuǐ?
什么时间上热水?

Please write that down.
Qǐng bǎ nàge xiěxiàlái.
请把那个写下来.

The no-tipping policy has also gradually broken down in the luxury hotels, where the Western-style ambience has somehow induced guests and workers to revive the custom.

Where's a telephone?
Diànhuà zài nǎr?
电话在哪儿?

Where's the dining room?
Cāntīng zài nǎr?
餐厅在哪儿?

Do you sell stamps?
Nǐzhàr mài yóupiào ma?
你这儿卖邮票吗?

Can you mail these?
Nǐ bǎ zhèxiē yóu zǒu hǎoma?
你把这些邮走好吗?

Do you have a safe?
Nǐ zhàr yǒu méi yǒu báoxiǎnxiāng?
你这儿有没有保险箱?

Do you check luggage here?
Nǐ zhàr yǒu méi yǒu xínglǐ bǎoguān?
你这儿有没有行李保管?

Could you keep these?
Bǎ zhèxiē cún zài nǐzhàr hǎoma?
把这些存在你这儿好吗?

Please give me a receipt.
Qǐng géi wǒ zhāngshōujù.
请给我张收据.

As elsewhere, hotels in China generally supply sundries to their captive market at higher prices than those items sell for just outside. Take a stroll around the neighborhood and check things out. Mineral water, soda, beer, and food are usually cheaper and offered in greater variety outside.

Where is a **grocery store?**
Shūcài shuíguǒdiàn zài nǎr?
蔬菜水果店在哪儿?

liquor store	*jiǔdiàn*	酒店
good restaurant	*hǎo cāntīng*	好餐厅
cheap restaurant	*piányìde cāntīng*	便宜的 餐厅
bank	*yínháng*	银行
post office	*yóujú*	邮局
book store	*shūdiàn*	书店
CITS office	*Zhōngguó Guójì Lǚyóu Gōngsì*	中国国际 旅遊公司
Public Security Bureau	*Gōngānjú*	公安局
Friendship Store	*Yǒuyì Shángdiàn*	友谊商店

Is there a **bus stop** nearby?
Fùjìn yǒu méi yǒu qìchēzhàn?
附近有没有汽车站?

train station	*huǒchēzhàn*	火车站
subway station	*dìtiězhàn*	地铁站
taxi stand	*chūzū chēzhàn*	出租车站
park	*gōngyuán*	公园

If you plan to wander far, be sure to get a business
card from your hotel, or have the name and address
written down in Chinese for you

Are there any **interesting sights** nearby?
Fùjìn yǒu méi yǒu yóulǎnqū?
附近有没有遊览区

local temples	*dìfāng sìmiào*	地方寺庙
famous	*yǒumíngde*	有名的
restaurants	*cāntīng*	餐厅
exhibit halls	*zhánlánguǎn*	展览馆
museums	*bówùguǎn*	博物馆
public parks	*gōngyuán*	公园

Do you have a name card for this hotel?
Nǐ yǒu méi yǒu zhèijiā fàndiànde míngxìnpiàn?
你有没有这家饭店的名信片?

Please write down the name and address.
Qíng bǎ míngzi, dìzhǐ xiěxiàlái.
请把名字, 地址写下来.

I'd like to go to this place.   (Show map, address)
Wó xiǎngqù zhèige dìfāng.
我想去这个地方.

Is it far? Can I walk?
Yuǎnma? Zǒuzhe qù xíngma?
远吗?走着去行吗?

How much will it cost?
Yào huā duōshǎo qián?
要花多少钱?

Although gradually casting off its Communist prudishness, China still offers little in the way of nightlife. Tourist hotel bars and discos are open to foreigners, but are expensive. Local discos and social gatherings may refuse you entry, but are worth a try. Halls equipped with Las Vegas-type gambling machines and other amusements are beginning to appear, but you must be a hard-core smoker to be able to stand them for any length of time. Ask about performances scheduled for foreign groups. If all else fails, bustling night markets are the best places for people watching.

Is there a **disco** nearby?
Fùjìn yǒu méi yǒu gēwǔtīng?
附近有没有歌舞厅？

bar	*jiǔbā*	酒吧
movie theater	*diànyǐngyuàn*	电影院
night market	*yèshì*	夜市

Are there any **musical performances** tonight?
Jīntiān wǎnshàng yǒu méi yǒu yīnyuèhuì?
令天晚上有没有音乐会？

theater performances	*xìjù*	戏剧
Peking opera performances	*jīngjù*	京剧
musical performances	*gēwǔ*	歌舞
acrobatic performances	*zájì*	杂技

Where can I buy tickets?
Wǒ zài nǎr kéyǐ mǎidào piàozi?
我在哪儿可以买到票子？

Getting In and Out

Most travelers to China enter the country through Beijing (Peking) or Hong Kong; Beijing receives most of the group tourists arriving to visit the ancient capitals of the north; Hong Kong hosts more of the individual travelers, the backpacking crowd who proceed up the Pearl river to Guangzhou (Canton).

Entering and leaving China used to be a tremendous hassle, with the Chinese and Communist love of bureaucratic order combining to make the paperwork scrutiny an excruciating process. Nowadays, however, entry and exit formalities have become confusingly lax. Three forms are still distributed on incoming flights: a customs declaration form; an entry/exit form; and a health/quarantine form.

The first is theoretically important and should be held on to and presented when you leave the country; on it you are supposed to declare the money and valuables you are carrying into China. You should certainly list anything which, if lost or stolen, you might need a record of or police report on to make an insurance claim later. At the same time, do not dispose of anything (except your money!), listed on the form, e.g., an inexpensive camera that quits on you; these items may be checked against the form when you leave China. In fact, however, this form is nowadays often ignored. Part of the second form is clipped into your passport, to be signed and removed when you exit China; it is important for individual travelers (those not on a group visa). The third, quarantine, form is roundly ignored; as a matter of fact, there's usually no one around to collect it.

After clearing immigration and customs, those on group tours will meet a representative of CITS (China International Travel Service, or *Lüxíngshè*) the official "host" of tourists visiting China. (If you are not contacted by someone, check at the CITS counter at the airport or train station.) He or she should have some transportation arranged to take you to your hotel. Individual travelers are on their own at this point, and will need the words and phrases on pp. 48–51 to get into town and find suitable accommodations.

In spite of the present laxness in entry formalities, exiting China can still be a problem. While group members are generally waved through customs, individual travelers may be subject to close scrutiny, especially any items that might appear to be antiques. It is best to hang on to receipts for all purchases and transactions. The Chinese love official paperwork; presenting a wad of receipts and a smile will often get you through. Above all, save at least one receipt for exchanged currency; it will be needed to exchange your Chinese money back into Hong Kong or U.S. dollars (usually the only choices). Note that if you are flying to Hong Kong, the weight allowance for domestic air transport (currently 20 kilos), will be adhered to; overloaded departing tourists are a good source of revenue.

Getting Around

China has all the transportation possibilities one would expect of a huge, continental country, from pedicabs to steam trains to Yangtze River cruise boats. Below are some general pointers to help you get around town. Note, however, that procedures for using the same type of vehicle often vary from city to city. See "Fingertips" on p. 78 for information on travel between cities.

bicycle *zìxíngchē* 自行车, p. 64
Chinese cities are vast and tourists sights can be far-flung. By far the best way to get around is to join the Chinese, on a bicycle. Rentals are available in most cities, usually near hotels; ask *Zài nǎr néng zū zìxíngchē?*, "Where can I rent a bicycle?" Half-day, whole-day, and multiple-day rentals are usually possible, and rates are reasonable. You will have to leave a deposit, or some I.D. that you can convince the shop is invaluable to you; leaving your passport is not recommended (but an old one will work). Chinese bikes are not grand touring machines, but one-speed utilitarian models (with great names, like "Flying Pigeon"); get there early for the best choice and check out the tires, brakes, and the lock. The bike parking areas that you see around town will sometimes not take you if the lock does not work. (Run by tough old grandmothers, they issue a receipt for a bike left under their care and watch it while you're gone.)

Try to remember something distinctive about your bike; there are probably ten million more just like it. Above all, ride calmly and defensively.

public bus *gōnggòng qìchē* 公共汽车, p. 65
The bus is the best transportation bargain in China, although what you save in *rénmínbì*, you certainly pay for in waiting time and crowd hassles. You'll need a local bus map and should do a little pre-boarding planning, including having your destination written out in Chinese. Once you choose the route number and find your stop, be prepared for the real Great Leap Forward; boarding can demand physical strength and creative elbow work. The good news is, for the extremely budget-minded, is that the ticket-seller on board will often not be able to get to you through the crowd. If she does, hold out a few *jiǎo*, point to your destination on the bus map, and she'll make the change. When the bus is not crowded, you usually purchase your ticket right after you board.

taxi *chūzū qìchē* 出租汽车, p. 66
Although metered taxis cruising the streets are common in large cities, taxis elsewhere are more commonly dealt with as are hired cars in the West: you arrange for them and agree on the fare before starting out. Most tourist hotels have taxi desks, where single trips, half-day, or full-day hires can be arranged. If you're at a restaurant or shop, ask someone to call for you. As with all negotiating in China, the important thing is to settle the amount before starting out. Write it down if need be.

pedicab *sānlúnchē* 三轮车
auto pedicab *sānlún mótuóchē* 三轮摩托车, p. 67
These vehicles and their drivers are found outside hotels, near bus and train stations, at major intersections, and around main tourist spots. As with hired cars, settle the fare before starting out; write it down and get it agreed upon.

day tours *yírìyóu* 一日遊, p. 68
Many important Chinese monuments, tombs in particular, are located well outside city centers, and a grueling round-trip ride on a public bus to see them could spoil the day. A better bet might be to join a one-day tour, usually with a guide and lunch, or at least a lunch stop, included. These are usually booked through hotels; at a luxury tourist hotels, services will naturally be better and prices higher. If budget is a big factor, join a Chinese group. (If you would like to listen to the guide and are a Mandarin speaker, make sure you aren't assigned a Hong Kong group.) If you have your own group of two to four, consider hiring a taxi for the day.

subway *dìtiě* 地铁, p. 70
Only Beijing has an extensive operating subway at present. Open from 5:00 till 10:30, the system (actually two unconnected lines) charges a flat fare for any distance, and is far speedier, although just as crowded, as buses. Shanghai has part of its newly built subway open.

For more expressions relating to location and direction, see p. 29.

How do I get to this place?
Dào zhège dìfāng zěnme zǒu?
到这个地方怎么走？

What's the best way to get there?
Qù nàr zuìhǎode bànfǎ shì shénme?
去那儿最好的办法是什么？

How far is it?
Lízhèr duō yuǎn?
离这儿多远？

How long will it take?
Yào zǒu duō jiǔ?
要走多久？

Is it difficult to find?
Nán zhǎoma?
难找吗？

Please show me on the map.
Qǐng zài dìtúshàng zhí gěi wǒ kànma.
请在地图上指给我看吗.

Please write it down in Chinese.
Qǐng yòng Zhōngwén xiěgěi wǒ kànma.
请用中文写给我看吗.

Can you arrange some transportation there?
Nǐ kéyǐ zài nàr ānpái yíxià chēpiào ma?
你可以在那儿安排一下车票吗？

Many Chinese do not know about bike rentals to foreigners, so don't take at face value the first assertion that there is no rental available.

Where can I rent a bicycle?
Wǒ zài nǎr kéyǐ jièdào yíliàng zìxíngchē?
我在哪儿可以借到一辆自行车？

I want to rent a bicycle.
Wǒ xiǎngjiè yíliàng zìxíngchē.
我想借一辆自行车．

How much is it for **an hour?**
Yígè zhōngtóu duōshǎo qián?
一个钟头多少钱？

half-day	*bàntiān*	半天
a day	*yìtiān*	一天
two days	*liǎngtiān*	两天

How much is the deposit?
Yājīn duōshǎo?
压金多少？

Where is bicycle parking?
Zìxíngchē cúnchēchù zài nǎr?
自行车存车处在哪儿？

Please write down the address of this shop.
Qíng bǎ zhège diànde dìzhǐ xiěyíxià.
请把这个店的地址写一下．

What time do you close?
Nín shénme shíjiān guānmén?
您什么时间关门？

Assuming you have done your homework and are on the right bus, the main consideration here is figuring out where to get off. You can get some help from the ticket seller, but this could be tough if the bus is crowded, which is usual.

Does bus number [NUMBER] stop here?
[NUMBER] hào gōnggòng qìchē zài zhàr tíng ma?
[NUMBER]号公共汽车在这儿停吗?

Does this bus go to [PLACE]?
Zhèliàng gōnggòng qìchē qù [PLACE] ma?
这辆公共汽车去[PLACE]吗?

I want to go here. Is this the right bus?
Wǒ xiǎngqù zhàr. Shì zuò zhèliàng qìchē ma?
我想去这儿. 是坐这辆汽车吗?

I want to go to [PLACE].
Wǒ xiǎngqù [PLACE].
我想去[PLACE].

I want to get off here.
Wǒ xiǎng zài zhàr xiàchē.
我想在这儿下车.

Would you tell me where to get off?
Nín néngfǒu gàosù wǒ zài nǎr xiàchē?
您能否告诉我在哪儿下车?

How many stops is it to [PLACE]?
Dào [PLACE] yào zuò jǐzhàn?
到[PLACE]要坐几站?

Half-day sightseeing trips by taxi can be quite economical for groups of four or fewer, especially compared with CITS cars, which come with a guide whether desired on not. Taxis are especially good for destinations out of town, in place of what could be a grueling round trip by bus.

I want to go here.   (Showing map or address)
Wó xiǎngqù zhàr.
我想去这儿.

I want to go to [PLACE].
Wǒ xiǎngqù [PLACE].
我想去[PLACE].

We want to go to these places.
Wǒmen xiǎngqù zhè jǐge dìfāng.
我们想去这几个地方.

I want you to wait. I want you to bring me back.
Qǐng nín děngděng. Qǐng nín bá wǒ dài huíqù.
请您等等. 请您把我带回去.

I'll be there about **one** hour.   (Numbers, p. 22)
*Wǒ dàyuē **yíge** zhōngtóu jiù dào.*
我大约一个钟头就到.

How much will it cost?
Zhèi yào duōshǎo qián?
这要多少钱?

How much for **a half day?**   (Time, p. 30)
Bàntiān *duōshǎo qián?*
半天多少钱?

a full day	*zhěngtiān*	整天
two hours	*liǎngge zhōngtóu*	两个钟头

Pedicab drivers seem to have adopted the scam of fare-raising as a universal *modus operandi;* it is thus even more imperative to settle the fare with them before starting off, preferably through agreement on a written figure. If you are hassled, don't argue; just laugh, put the agreed upon fare on the vehicle, and walk away, toward a crowd.

How much will it cost?
Yào huā duōshǎo qián?
要花多少钱?

That's for both of us, right?
Nà bāokuò wǒmén liǎngge, duì bú duì?
那包括我们俩个, 对不对?

How much to take us and bring us back?
Dài wǒmén láihuí duōshǎo qián?
带我们来回多少钱?

Stop here, please.
Qǐng zài zhàr tíng.
请在这儿停.

Wait here, please.
Qǐng zài zhàr děng.
请在这儿等.

This is all I will pay.
Wó zhǐ néng fù zhème duō.
我只能负这么多.

Unless your tour provides an English-speaking guide, you may wish to sightsee on your own and return to the bus when it's time to leave.

Do you have any tours to [PLACE]?
Nín yǒu méi yǒu qù [PLACE] de lǚyóutuán?
您有没有去 [PLACE] 的旅遊团?

We want to see [PLACE].
Wǒmén xiǎngkàn [PLACE].
我们想看 [PLACE].

Is the tour offered every day?
Nǐmén měitiān dōu dài lǚyóutuán ma?
你们每天都带旅遊团吗?

How much time will we spend there?
Wǒmén yào zài nàr dāi duōjiǔ?
我们要在那儿呆多久?

What time does the tour start?
Lǚyóu jídiǎn kāishǐ?
旅遊几点开始?

Where do we join the tour?
Wǒmén zài nǎr jíhé?
我们在那儿集合?

What time will we get back?
Wǒmén shénme shíjiān huílái?
我们什么时间回来?

If you elect to leave the group, be sure to accompany the leader past any ticket-takers if admission is included, and find out when and from where your group is scheduled to depart.

Is admission included?
Rùchǎngquàn bāokuòle ma?
入场券包括了吗？

Is lunch included?
Wǔfàn bāokuòle ma?
午饭包括了吗？

Is there a guide?
Yǒu méi yǒu dǎoyóu?
有没有导遊？

Does the guide speak English?
Dǎoyóu jiǎng Yīngwén ma?
导遊讲英文吗？

How much is it altogether?
Yígòng duōshǎo qián?
一共多少钱？

What time do we have to be back on the bus?
Wǒmén jídiǎn huídào qìchē shàng?
我们几点回到汽车上？

Where will the bus be parked?
Qìchē tíng zài nǎr?
汽车停在哪儿？

Beijing actually has two subway lines, a Circle Line running around the central city and an East-West line running out to the western suburbs. They are not connected. The Circle Line is very convenient for Beijing sightseeing.

What's the closest subway stop to [PLACE]?
Qù [PLACE] *de dìtiě zài nǎr?*
去[PLACE]的地铁在哪儿?

Where's the subway station?
Dìtiě zài nǎr?
地铁在哪儿?

Is this the Circle Line?
Zhèi shì Huánchéng Xiàn ma?
这是环城线吗?

Is this the East-West Line?
Zhèi shì Dōngxī Xiàn ma?
这是东西线吗?

How many stops to [PLACE]?
Qù [PLACE] *zuò jǐzhàn?*
去[PLACE]坐几站?

Is this the stop for [PLACE]?
Zhèi zhàn shì bú shì [PLACE]?
这站是不是[PLACE]?

Could you tell me when we get to [PLACE]?
Qǐng gàosù wǒ shénme shíjiān dào [PLACE]?
请告诉我什么时间到[PLACE]?

Fares vary depending on class (there is no first class, but there is a second, third, and fourth class). There is time to stroll in town at some of the stops; be sure to ask what time the boat leaves.

I want to go to [PLACE].
Wǒ xiǎngqù [PLACE].
我想去[PLACE].

I want a **second-class** ticket.
Wǒ xiǎngyào **èrděngcāng** *piào.*
我想要二等仓票.

third-class	*sānděngcāng*	三等仓
fourth-class	*sìděngcāng*	四等仓

How much is it?
Duōshǎo qián?
多少钱?

Where is the restaurant?
Fànguǎn zài nǎr?
饭馆在哪儿?

What time do we get to [PLACE]?
Wǒmén shénme shíjiān dào [PLACE]?
我们什么时间到[PLACE]?

How long will we stop?
Wǒmén tíng duōjiǔ?
我们停多久?

What time does the boat leave?
Chuán jídiǎn kāi?
船几点开?

In China, where things go wrong more often than seems normal, it is best not to test the system; get to the airport at least full hour before your flight. There are modest departure taxes (50 *yuán* at present) at all Chinese airports.

I want to fly to [PLACE].
Wó xiǎngzuò fēijī qù [PLACE].
我想坐飞机去[PLACE].

What time do you have flights?
Nǐmén yǒu jídiǎnde fēijī?
你们有几点的飞机?

I want to leave **tomorrow**.   (Days, p. 32)
*Wó xiǎng **míngtiān** zǒu.*
我想明天走.

I want to leave around **noon**.   (Time, p. 34)
*Wó xiǎng **zhōngwǔ** zuǒyòu zǒu.*
我想中午左右走.

What time is the earliest flight?
Zuìzǎode fēijī jídiǎn?
最早的飞机几点?

What time is the latest flight?
Zuìwǎnde fēijī jídiǎn?
最晚的飞机几点?

I want a first-class ticket.
Wó xiǎngyào yìděngcāng piào.
我想要一等仓票.

I want an economy-class ticket.
Wó xiǎngyào èrděng zuòcì piào.
我想要二等座次票.

Flying in China is fun, with stewardesses distributing a stream of candies and plastic knickknacks (wallets, key chains, shoe-shine kits). On the other hand, the food will cause you to recall fondly the great meals you were served on planes back home.

I'd like to buy a ticket now.
Wǒ xiǎng xiànzài mǎi zhāng piào.
我想现在买张票.

I like to make a reservation.
Wǒ xiǎng yùyuē.
我想预约.

How much is the fare?
Piàojià duōshǎo?
票价多少?

How much is the departure tax?
Jīchǎngfèi duōshǎo?
机场费多少?

How long is the flight?
Fēixíng shíjiān duōcháng?
飞行时间多长?

What time does the flight leave?
Fēijī jídiǎn qǐfēi?
飞机几点起飞?

What time does the flight arrive?
Fēijī jídiǎn dào dá?
飞机几点到达?

Which gate is it?
Nǎge rùkǒu?
哪个入口?

You can generally avoid the hassle of the train station by asking at your hotel whether tickets can be gotten for you. Or you can get them at a CITS office, of course, at some markup. You can also buy a platform ticket and buy your trip ticket after you board the train, although you risk being stuck in unreserved hard seat.

I want to go to [PLACE].
Wó xiăngqù [PLACE].
我想去[PLACE].

I want to leave **tomorrow**.   (Days, p. 32)
*Wó xiăng **míngtiān** zŏu.*
我想明天走.

What time are there trains?
Jídiăn yóu huŏchē?
几点有火车?

What time is the earliest train?
Zuìzăode huŏchē jídiăn?
最早的火车几点?

What time is the latest train?
Zuìwănde huŏchē jídiăn?
最晚的火车几点?

I want a reserved **hard-seat** ticket.
*Wó xiăng yùyuē yìzhāng **yìngzuò** piào.*
我想预约一张硬座票.

hard-sleeper	*yìngwò*	硬卧
soft-seat	*ruănzuò*	软座
soft-sleeper	*ruănwò*	软卧

Train food varies from adequate to awful, but there are lots of vendors at station stops hawking anything you might want. Stations are marked with *pinyin* names as well as Chinese characters, so you can keep track of your journey on a map.

How much is the ticket?
Piàozi duōshǎo qián?
票子多少钱？

How long is the trip?
Lǚchéng duōcháng shíjiān?
旅程多长时间？

What time does the train leave?
Huǒchē jídiǎn kāi?
火车几点开？

What time does the train arrive?
Huǒchē jídiǎn dào?
火车几点到？

Which stop is this?
Zhèi zhàn shì nǎr?
这站是哪儿？

How many stops until [PLACE]?
Dào [PLACE] háiyǒu jǐzhàn?
到[PLACE]还有几站？

Where's the dining car?
Cānchē zài nǎr?
餐车在哪儿？

I'd like to upgrade my ticket.
Wó xiǎng tígāo wǒde zuò piào děngcì.
我想提高我的座票等次．

There is little space for luggage on long-distance buses, so travel light, although you should bring some snacks with you. The buses typically stop for food at fairly grungy truck-stop-type joints.

I want to go to [PLACE].
Wǒ xiǎngqù [PLACE].
我想去[PLACE].

I want to leave **today**.   (Days, p. 32)
Wǒ xiǎng jīntiān zǒu.
我想今天走.

What time are there buses?
Jídiǎn yǒu qìchē?
几点有汽车?

What time is the next bus?
Xiàyítàng qìchē jídiǎn?
下一趟汽车几点.

Is there an overnight bus?
Yǒu méi yǒu yèjiān qìchē?
有没有夜间汽车?

Please give me a ticket.
Qǐng gěi wǒ yìzhāng piào.
请给我一张票.

I'd like to sit close to the front.
Wǒ xǐhuān zuòzài qiánmiàn.
我喜欢坐在前面.

How much is the ticket?
Piàozi duōshǎo qián?
票子多少钱?

Buses are subject to accidents and breakdowns, so they are not suitable for those on strict schedules. Note that some buses continue traveling through the night, with or without changing drivers.

How long is the trip?
Lǚtú yǒu duōjiǔ?
旅途有多久?

What time does the bus leave?
Qìchē jídiǎn kāichē?
汽车几点开车?

What time will we get there?
Wǒmén jídiǎn dào nǎr?
我们几点到那儿?

Where are we now?
Wǒmén xiànzài zài nǎr?
我们现在在哪儿?

How long will we stop here?
Wǒmén zài zhàr tíng duōjiǔ?
我们在这儿停多久?

When is the next stop?
Xiàzhàn shénme shíjiān dào?
下站什么时间到?

Will we stop overnight?
Wǒmén guòyè ma?
我们过夜吗?

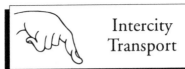

Intercity Transport

boat *chuán* 船, p.71
Tourists are likely to travel by long-distance boat only if they cruise the Yangzi River. The most popular route is the three-day trip downstream from Chongqing to Wuhan (or a five-day trip upstream). If you want only to see the Three Gorges (Sanxia), the two-day trip from Chongqing to Yichang is sufficient; at Yichang you can get a train.

plane *fēijī* 飞机, p.72
China's air transport system is sorely overtaxed, and tickets are not always easy to get, even paying the mandatory 75% surcharge for foreigners. If you plan to leave a city by air, it is best to make arrangements when you arrive. The fee is modest, 10%, if you cancel more than 24 hours in advance. Reservations are accepted, but since you can be bumped by some VIP at the last minute, or your reservation conveniently lost when the plane fills up, it is better to purchase the actual ticket. Baggage limits of 20 kilos for economy class and 30 for first class seem often to be ignored, except on select routes (e.g., Lhasa to Chengdu) where making overburdened foreigners pay up seems to be an important component of the local economy. Baggage allowances are strictly adhered to on international CAAC flights; on the other hand, carry-on luggage is rarely checked or weighed.

train *huǒchē* 火车, p. 74
China has an extensive rail system, serving all areas
except Tibet and far-western Xinjiang; trains are
reasonably priced and fairly easy to use. They are,
however, like all Chinese transportation, packed.
In the past, paying a modest amount extra (even
with the surcharge for foreigners) could get you a
ticket a class away from the madding crowd; nowadays, however, many more Chinese have money
and are traveling, and competition for better
accommodations is fierce. As with plane tickets,
it's a good idea to take care of your onward transportation when you first arrive at a city. The two
classes of carriage, hard and soft, are further
divided into seats or sleepers. Hard seats are the
cheapest, and although the seats are actually
padded, it is difficult to take more than eight
hours or so with the crowds, garbage, noise, and
smoke. You can travel with a reserved seat or unreserved; you can also ask the train staff for an
upgrade, although this obviously can be done
only on a space available basis.

long-distance bus *chángtú qìchē* 长途汽车, p. 76
Long-distance buses are another very economical
way of getting around the country, and you really
see a lot more of life in the Chinese countryside
than you can from the train. Buses usually leave
from yards located on the edges of smaller towns,
or central depots in bigger cities. Tickets reserve
you a numbered seat; the ride is naturally smoother
if you can get a middle or front seat.

Getting Acquainted

Fingertip Chinese is designed as a phrase book rather than a language text, so it will not help you through a dialogue on, say, the philosophical differences between Confucius and his follower, Mencius. However, Chinese are quite interested in life in other countries and under the right circumstances (see "Fingertips," p.104) will be happy to chat with you about fairly trivial topics. Their queries to you will likely be along the lines of those listed below. Remember that there is no intention of offending; money and family life are considered practical matters that the Chinese are interested in finding out about.

What's your name?
Nín guì xìng?
您贵姓?
Literally, "Your honorable surname?," this question is answered by saying *Wǒ xìng* [SURNAME]. You can, of course, simply state your last name, and if it is important that it be understood or remembered, write it down. Bilingual name cards are a must for anyone doing business in China.

Where are you from?
Nǐ shì cóng nǎr láide?
你是从哪儿来的?
Chinese have their own stereotypes of foreigners and their countries, and are more comfortable if they can relate you to one of them. The easiest

response to this is to state your nationality (p. 86), e.g., *Měiguórén* ("American").

How old are you?
Nǐ duō dà?
你多大?
Note that this is different from the question used to ask the ages of children, which is *Nǐ jǐ suì?* Either question, however, can be answered by using the numbers on p. 22, followed by *suì* ("year"), for example, *Èrshíyī suì* ("Twenty-one").

Are you married?
Nǐ jiéhūnle ma?
你结婚了吗?
Questions of marriage and family typically seem to hold a much stronger interest for Asians than for Westerners. *Jiéhūnle* ("Married") or *Hái méi ne* ("Not yet") are appropriate answers.

Do you have children?
Nǐ yǒu háizile ma?
你有孩子吗?
The answer to this is either *Yǒu* ("Are," meaning "Yes") or *Méi yǒu* ("Aren't," meaning "No"). See p. 90 for vocabulary to describe family members.

Do you have a boyfriend (girlfriend)?
Nǐ yǒu méi yǒu nánpéngyou (nǚpéngyou)?
你有没有男朋友(女朋友)?
This could be a innocent follow-up question or an inquiry into matchmaking possibilities. Answer accordingly, either *Yǒu* ("There is," meaning "Yes") or *Méi yǒu* ("There isn't," meaning "No").

How much money do you make?
Nǐ zhèng duōshǎo qián?
你挣多少钱？
Although regarded by Westerners as overly intrusive, this question addresses what is to Chinese an important and practical matter. If you don't wish to state a specific amount, you can deflect the question with answers such as *Bú gòu!* ("Not enough!").

How much rent do you pay?
Nǐ fángzū shì duōshǎo?
你房租是多少钱？
A variant of this is "How much does a house cost?" As Westerners like to be impressed with stories of $300 melons offered in Tokyo department stores, Chinese like to hear of the huge sums we spend on basic necessities in the West. I sometimes try to explain that these sums are relative to income, and that the Chinese, in fact, spend a smaller percentage of their income on housing. However, I have never had much luck with this, and generally wind up offering a rather lame general statement: *Fángzū hěn guì!* ("Rent is expensive!").

Cultural Considerations

Friendships with Chinese can be lifetime affairs undergoing many evolutions and ultimately working on any of many levels. One generally receives, even from new Chinese acquaintances, a genuinely warm and friendly welcome. Chinese are proud of their nation and its cultural contributions to the world, and happy to help you have the best time possible while sojourning among them. If you ask for more than the most perfunctory assistance, however, you should be aware of some cultural differences that may confuse issues. The same Chinese who will "frankly" discuss politics and personal finances with you may not "frankly" admit to you that what you have requested is impossible. This is not a matter of evasiveness as much as it is saving "face"; the rules of Chinese interpersonal relationships are geared to avoiding those moments when the individual, in the presence of others, must appear either to refuse or to fail to deliver. The evasive answer must be taken to mean what it would to other Chinese, "No way."

At the same time, Chinese pride themselves on their *guānxi*, or "connections," people who either owe them favors or through whom they can get things done. Thus, having expressed a particular interest, you might find yourself treated to a tour of a facility normally closed to the public, or a meeting with a high official not otherwise accessible. Be cognizant of the level of hospitality you are receiving and be prepared to return the favor—perhaps not right away but at some future date, when a friend or relative of your new Chinese acquaintance comes to visit your country.

For greetings which can also serve as conversational openers, see page 20.

What's your name?
Nín jiào shénme?
您叫什么？

What's going on?
Nín jìnkuàng rúhé?
您近况如何？

Beautiful day, isn't it.
Jīntiān tiān zhēn hǎo.
今天天真好.

Do you speak English?
Nín jiǎng Yīngwén mā?
您讲英文吗？

How cute. How old is she (he)?
Zhēn dòurén xǐhuān. Duōdàle?
真逗人善欢. 多大了？

Can I take a photo?
Zhào zhāngxiàng, xíngma?
照张象, 行吗？

Do you like sightseeing?
Ní xǐhuān jiāoyóu ma?
您善欢郊遊吗？

This is really interesting, isn't it?
Zhēn hén yǒu yìsi, duì bú duì?
真很有意思, 对不对？

Discussing a particular item or object or place is probably the best way to get an extended conversation started. Rest assured that there will be much to ask about.

What's this?
Zhè shì shénme?
这是什么？

What do you call it in Chinese?
Zhège Zhōngwén zěnme jiǎng?
这个中文怎么讲？

Do you know what it's called in English?
Nǐ zhīdào zhège Yīngwén zěnme shuō ma?
你知道这个英文怎么说吗？

What is it for?
Zhèi shì gàn shénme yòngde?
这是干什么用的？

How is it used?
Zhèige zěnme yòng?
这个怎么用？

What is it made of?
Zhè shì shénme zuòde?
这是什么做的？

Do you eat this?
Nǐ chī zhège ma?
你吃这个吗？

Is it good?
Hǎochī ma?
好吃吗？

New Chinese acquaintances will naturally be curious about who you are, where you are from, your work, interests, and family.

My name is [NAME].
Wǒ jiào [NAME].
我叫[NAME].

I'm **American.**
*Wǒ shì **Měiguó rén.***
我是美国人.

Australian	*Àodàlìyà rén*	澳大利亚人
English	*Yīngguó rén*	英国人
Canadian	*Jiānádà rén*	加拿大人

I'm from **New York.**
*Wǒ cóng **Niuyuē** lái.*
我从纽约来.

Sydney	*Xīní*	悉尼
London	*Lúndūn*	伦敦
Montreal	*Méngtèlìěr*	蒙特利尔

I'm a **teacher.**
*Wǒ shì **jiàoshī.***
我是教师.

student	*xuéshēng*	生学
businessman	*shāngrén*	商人
doctor	*yīshēng*	医生
engineer	*gōngchéngshī*	工程师
journalist	*jìzhě*	记者
lawyer	*lùshī*	律师
salesman	*tuīxiāoyuán*	推销员

These patterns and substitutions can be used to state your interests in various activities and subjects or, if you are a student, your major.

I'm interested in **history.**
Wǒ duì lìshǐ gǎn xìngqù.
我对历史感兴趣

I'm studying **architecture.**
Wǒ zài xué jiànzhù.
我在学建筑.

archaeology	*káogǔxúe*	考古学
art	*měishù*	美术
computers	*diàn nǎu*	电脑
design	*shèjì*	设计
economics	*jīngjì*	经济
history	*lìshǐ*	历史
literature	*wénxué*	文学
mathematics	*shùxué*	术学
philosophy	*zhéxué*	哲学
physics	*wùlì*	物理
science	*kēxué*	科学

I enjoy **reading.**
Wǒ ài kànshū.
我爱看书.

music	*yīnyuè*	音乐
sports	*tǐyù*	体育
movies	*diànyǐng*	电影
theater	*jùchǎng*	剧场
photography	*shèyǐng*	摄影
travel	*lǚyóu*	旅游
cooking	*pēngtiáo*	烹调

The following can be used to express more precisely your taste in music, movies, books, and film.

I like **classical music.**
*Wó xǐhuān **gúdiǎn yīnyuè.***
我善欢古典音乐.

rock 'n' roll	*yáobǎiyuè*	摇摆乐
country	*xiāngcūnyīnyuè*	乡村音乐
jazz	*juéshìyuè*	爵士乐

I play the violin.
*Wǒ lá **xiǎotíqín.***
我拉小提玲.

guitar	*jítā*	吉他
piano	*gāngqín*	钢玲
saxophone	*sàkèsīguǎn*	萨克斯管
clarinet	*dānhuángguǎn*	单簧管

I like to read **fiction.**
*Wó xǐhuān kàn **xiǎoshuō.***
我善欢看小说.

non-fiction	*fēi xiǎoshuō wénxué*	非小说文学
poetry	*shīgē*	诗歌
mysteries	*shénmìjù*	神秘剧

I like **historical** movies.
*Wó xǐhuān **lìshǐ** diànyǐng.*
我善欢历史电影.

documentaries	*jìlùpiān*	记录片
comedies	*xǐjù*	善剧
musicals	*yīnyuèjù*	音乐剧
thrillers	*jīngxiǎnpiān*	惊险片

Chinese are very interested in sports, and will want to learn of your interests, if any. And, of course, they will be pleased if you express an interest in their culture.

I like **baseball.**
Wó xǐhuān bàngqíu.
我善欢棒球.

soccer	*zúqíu*	足球
American football	*Měishì zúqíu*	美式足球
basketball	*lánqíu*	篮球
bicycling	*zìxíngchē*	自行车
golf	*gāoěrfū*	高尔夫
swimming	*yóuyǒng*	游泳
rugby	*gánlǎnqíu*	橄榄球
tennis	*wǎngqíu*	网球

I'm interested in Chinese **architecture.**
Wó xǐhuān Zhōngguó jiànzhù.
我善欢中国建筑.

business	*shāngyè*	商业
cinema	*diànyǐng shìyè*	电影事业
crafts	*gōngyì*	工艺
culture	*wénhuà*	文化
dance	*wúdǎo*	舞蹈
food	*shípǐn*	食品
history	*lìshǐ*	史历
literature	*wénxué*	文学
martial arts	*wǔshù*	武术
music	*yīnyuè*	音乐
theater	*xìjù*	戏剧

Chinese will curious about your family and your marital status. Again, questions that may seem prying are more likely the result of the typically strong Asian interest in these topics, as well the Chinese notion that Westerners tend to speak frankly even about personal matters.

I'm married. / I'm single.
Wǒ jiéhūnle. / *Wǒ dānshēn.*
我结婚了. 我单身.

We have **three children**.   (Numbers, p. 22)
Wǒmén yǒu sānge háizi.
我们有三个孩子.

two sons	*liǎngge érzi*	两个儿子
one daughter	*yīge nǚér*	一个女儿

I have a **younger brother**.
Wǒ yǒu ge dìdì.
我有个弟弟.

younger sister	*mèimèi*	妹妹
older brother	*gēge*	哥哥
older sister	*jiějiě*	姐姐

I'm the oldest son (daughter).
Wǒ shì dà érzi (nǚér).
我是大儿子(女儿).

I'm the youngest son (daughter).
Wǒ shì zuìdà de érzi (nǚér).
我是最大的儿子(女儿).

I'm an only son (daughter).
Wǒ shì dúshēng zǐ (nǚ).
我是独生子(女).

Chinese will be curious about what you are doing in their country, including the purpose of your trip and the details of your itinerary.

I'm here **on business**.
*Wǒ lái zhàr **jīngshāng**.*
我来这儿经商.

on vacation	*dùjià*	渡假
to study Chinese	*xué Zhōngwén*	学中文

I'll be here for **a few days**. (Time, p. 31)
*Wǒ yào zài zhàr zhù **jǐtiān**.*
我要在这儿住几天.

a week	*yìzhōu*	一周
two weeks	*liǎngzhōu*	两周

I came **three days ago**. (Time, p. 31)
*Wǒ **sāntiān qián** láide.*
我三天前来了.

three weeks	*sānzhōu*	三周
one month	*yíge yuè*	一个月

Yesterday I went to [PLACE].
Zuótiān wǒ qùle [PLACE].
昨天我去了[PLACE].

I'm on my way to [PLACE].
Wǒ zhèngyào qù [PLACE].
我正要去[PLACE].

I plan to go to [PLACE].
Wǒ jìhuà qù [PLACE].
我计划去[PLACE].

Chinese will be interested in your views on their country. How candid and precise you wish to be is up to you; below are some positive comments.

I find China fascinating.
Wǒ fāxiàn Zhōngguó tài yǐnrénle.
我发现中国太引人了.

The **Ming Tombs** were the most amazing.
***Shísān Líng** zuì zhuàng guān.*
十三陵最壮观.

Forbidden City	*Zǐjìn Chéng*	紫禁城
Palace Museum	*Gùgōng*	故宫
Great Wall	*Chángchéng*	长城
terra-cotta army	*bīngmǎ yǒng*	兵马俑
Lung Men caves	*Lóngmén shíkū*	龙门石窟
Suzhou gardens	*Sūzhōu línyuán*	苏州林园
Guilin scenery	*Guìlín shānshuǐ*	贵林山水

I love Chinese food.
Wǒ tèbié xǐhuān Zhōngguó shípǐn.
我特别善欢中国食品.

The people are very friendly.
Rénmén dōu hén yǒushàn.
人们都很友善.

The economy seems booming.
Jīngjì kànqǐlái hén xīngshèng.
经济看来很兴盛.

I definitely want to come back.
Wǒ dāngrán yuànyì zàilái.
我当然愿意再来.

On the other hand, more negative or controversial comments may make for more interesting exchanges.

Traffic is a nightmare.
Jiāotōng zǔsè lìngrén tóuténg.
交通组塞另人头疼.

People drive like lunatics.
Rénmén kāichē xiàng fēngle yíyàng.
人们开车象疯了一样.

Trains and buses are too crowded.
Huǒchē hé qìchē dōu tài jǐ.
火车和汽车都太挤.

People always push and shove.
Rénmén zǒngshì yòu tuī yòu sǎng.
人们总是又推又搡.

There's a great deal of pollution.
Wūrǎn tài yánzhòng.
污染太严重.

The cities seem quite crowded.
Chéngshì kànqǐlái dōu hěn jǐ.
城市看起来都很挤.

The countryside looks very poor.
Nóngcūn kànqǐlái hěn pínqióng.
农村看起来很贫穷.

Hotels for foreigners are too crowded.
Duì wàibīn kāifàngde fàndiàn tài jǐ.
对外宾开放的饭店太挤.

Foreigners always have to pay too much.
Wàibīn zǒngshì bù dé bù fù hěnduō qián.
外宾总是不得不负很多钱.

To express opinions it is useful to know some adjectives. These are actually stative verbs (see p. 40), but since Chinese verbs are not inflected for person, number, or tense, they are easy to use; they can stand alone as sentences, referring to topics that are understood, or they can be preceded by specific subjects.

It is/was...	It is/was very...	It isn't/wasn't...
good *hǎo* 好	*hén hǎo* 很好	*bù hǎo* 不好
cold *lěng* 冷	*hén lěng* 很冷	*bù lěng* 不冷
hot *rè* 热	*hǎo rè* 好热	*bú rè* 不热
expensive *guì* 贵	*hěn guì* 很贵	*bú guì* 不贵
cheap *piányì* 便宜	*hén piányì* 很便宜	*bù piányì* 不便宜
delicious *hǎochī* 好吃	*hén hǎochī* 很好吃	*bù hǎochī* 不好吃
convenient *fāngbiàn* 方便	*hěn fāngbiàn* 很方便	*bù fāngbiàn* 不方便

As an example of their versatility, *tài duō*, can be used to express "too much" to a street vendor trying to load you up with a pile of fruit, or "too high," in response to a suggested price.

It is/was...	It is/was very...	It isn't/wasn't...
big		
dà	*hén dà*	*bú dà*
大	很大	不大
small		
xiǎo	*hén xiǎo*	*bù xiǎo*
小	很小	不小
long		
cháng	*hěn cháng*	*bù cháng*
长	很长	不长
short		
duǎn	*hén duǎn*	*bù duǎn*
短	很短	不短
light		
qīng	*hěn qīng*	*bù qīng*
轻	很轻	不轻
heavy		
zhòng	*hěn zhòng*	*bú zhòng*
重	很重	不重
enough		
gòu	—	*bú gòu*
够	—	不够

Turnabout is fair play, and the best way to get a break from answering questions posed by your Chinese acquaintances is to ask some of your own.

What kind of work do you do?
Nǐ shì gàn shénmede?
你是干什么的?

Who do you work for?
Nǐ zài nǎjiā gōngsī zuòshì?
你在哪家公司做事?

Are you a student?
Nǐ shì xuéshēng ma?
你是学生吗?

What do you study?
Nǐ xué shénme?
你学什么?

What kind of job do you want to get?
Nǐ xiǎng zuò shénme?
你想做什么?

Are you originally from here?
Nǐ shìfǒu chūshēng zài zhàr?
你是否出生在这儿?

Where do you live?
Nǐ zài nǎr zhù?
你在哪儿住?

How much rent to you pay?
Nǐ fángzū duōshǎo?
你房租多少?

Don't feel awkward asking questions about home and family life; the Chinese will certainly ask you. Moreover, they may lead to an invitation to visit a home, a rare treat.

Are you married?
Nǐ jiéhūnle ma?
你结婚了吗？

How many children do you have?
Nǐ yǒu jǐge háizi?
你有几个孩子？

Do you come from a big family?
Nǐ shì láizì yígè dà jiātíng ma?
你是来自一个大家庭吗？

What are you interested in?
Nǐ xǐhuān shénme?
你善欢什么？

What do you like to do in your free time?
Nǐ xiánshí zuòxiē shénme?
你闲时做些什么？

What kind of movies do you like?
Nǐ xǐhuān kànshénme diànyǐng?
你善欢看什么电影？

Do you ever see Western movies?
Nǐ kànguò Xīfāng diànyǐng ma?
你看过西方电影吗？

What's your favorite Western movie?
Nǐ zuì xǐhuān nǎ bù Xīfāng diànyǐng?
你最善欢哪部西方电影吗？

Chinese are big sports fans, and especially interested in the Summer Olympics and Asian Games, in which their teams have been quite successful. Western music is popular, and the gift of a cassette tape by a new or popular group will be well received.

Which sports do you like to watch?
Nǐ xǐhuān názhǒng tǐyù xiàngmù?
你善欢哪种体育项目?

Which sports do you play?
Nǐ cóngshì názhǒng tǐyù huódòng?
你从事哪种体育浩动?

Do you watch the Olympics?
Nǐ kàn Àolínpǐkè yùndòngghuì ma?
你看奥林匹克运动会哪?

Do you like music?
Nǐ xǐhuān yīnyuè ma?
你善欢音乐吗?

What kind of music do you like?
Nǐ xǐhuān shénme yīnyuè?
你善欢什么音乐?

Do you listen to Western music?
Nǐ tīng Xīfāng yuèqǔ ma?
你听西方乐曲吗?

Who is your favorite singer?
Nǐ zuì xǐhuān nǎwèi gēshǒu?
你最善欢哪位歌手?

Do you play any instruments?
Nǐ huì názhǒng yuè qì?
你会哪种乐器?

Most Chinese are interested in travel, whether or not they have had the opportunity to do so.

Do you like to read?
Nǐ xǐhuān kànshū ma?
你善欢看书吗？

What kind of books do you like?
Nǐ xǐhuān kàn shénme shū?
你善欢看什么书吗？

Do you read any Western authors?
Nǐ dú bù dú Xīfāng zuòjiāde zuòpǐn?
你读不读西方作家的作品？

Which Western books or authors do you like?
Nǐ xǐhuān Xīfāng nǎ xiē zuòjiā hé zuòpǐn?
你善欢西方哪些作家和作品？

Have you ever traveled abroad?
Nǐ zài guówài lǚyóu guòma?
你在国外旅游过吗？

Have you traveled in China?
Nǐ zài Zhōngguó lǚyóu guòma?
你在中国旅游过吗？

Where did you go?
Nǐ qùguo nǎr?
你去过哪儿？

How did you like it?
Nǐ xǐhuān ma?
你善欢吗？

Where would you most like to travel to?
Nǐ zuì xǐhuān qù nǎr lǚyóu?
你最善欢去哪儿旅游？

While on a bus or train traveling to a place you haven't been, take the opportunity to get some information about it.

Have you ever been to [PLACE]?
Nǐ qùguo [PLACE] *ma?*
你去过[PLACE]吗?

What's it like?
Nàr shì shénme yàng?
哪是什么样?

What are the important sights to see?
Nǎrxiē fēngjǐngqū yīnggāi kànkàn?
哪些风景区应该看看?

What are some interesting things to do?
Dào nàr gàndiǎn shénme?
到那儿干点什么?

Are there any famous local products?
Nàr yǒuxiē shénme dìfāng fēngwèi?
那儿有些什么地方风味?

Are there any famous local dishes?
Nàge dìfāng shénme cài zuì yǒumíng?
那个地方什么菜最有名?

Can you recommend a good place to stay?
Nǐ néng bù néng jièshàoge hǎode zhùchù?
你能不能介绍个好的住处?

Is there a CITS office there?
Nàr yǒu Lǚxíngshè ma?
哪有旅行社吗?

Entertaining guests in China means offering them (actually, forcing on them) food and drink. If you find yourself in the position of guest, as you will inevitably be, keep in mind that the more you consume the happier your hosts will be.

I'd like to invite you to dinner tonight.
Jīntiān wǎnshàng wǒ qíng nǐ chī wǎnfàn.
今天晚上我请你吃晚饭.

Thank you very much.
Fēicháng gǎnxiè.
非常感谢.

To your health!   (Literally, "Dry glass!" a toast)
Gānbēi!
干杯!

Now about another toast?
Zài lái yìzhōng?
再来一盅?

No thanks. I'm full.
Bú yào, xièxiè. Wǒ chībǎole.
不要, 谢谢. 我吃饱了.

No thanks. I don't want to get too drunk.
Bú yào, xièxiè. Wǒ bù xiǎng hēde tài zuì.
不要, 谢谢. 我不想喝得太醉.

No thanks. I don't smoke.
Bú yào, xièxiè. Wǒ bù xīyān.
不要, 谢谢. 我不吸烟.

Thank you for inviting me.
Xièxiè nínde yāoqǐng.
谢谢您的约请.

The following expressions are useful for situations in which it is very important that you understand what is being said to you.

Sorry, I don't understand.
Duìbuqǐ, wǒ bù dǒng.
对不起, 我不懂.

Please say that again.
Qǐng zài shuō yíbiàn.
请再说一遍.

Please speak more slowly.
Qǐng jiǎng màn yìdiǎn.
请讲慢一点.

Can you say that in English?
Nín néng yòng Yīngwén shuō yíbiàn ma?
您能用英文请再说一遍吗?

Can you find it in this phrase book?
Zài zhèběn shūlǐ néng zhǎodào zhège cí ma?
在这本书里能找到这个词吗?

Can you translate for me?
Nín néng gěi wǒ fānyì yíxià ma?
您能给我翻译一下吗?

Sorry, my Chinese is really bad.
Duìbuqǐ, wǒde Zhōngwén shízài zāogāo.
对不起, 我的中文实在糟糕.

I agree. / I don't agree.
Wǒ tóngyì. / Wǒ bù tóngyì.
我同意. / 我不同意.

All conversations must come to an end. By all means consider favorably the possibility of an acquaintance blossoming into a friendship. If you decide to exchange addresses, do so with a realistic awareness of expectations on both sides.

Sorry, I don't speak Chinese.
Duìbuqǐ, wǒ bù jiǎng Zhōngwén.
对不起, 我不遘中文.

Sorry, I've got to go.
Duìbuqǐ, wó déi zǒule.
对不起, 我得走了.

Excuse me, I have to join my group.
Láojià, wó děi gēnshàng wǒde xiáozǔ.
劳驾, 我得跟上我的小组.

It was nice to meet you.
Yǒuxìng yú nǐ xiāngféng.
有幸与你相逢.

Here's my address.
Zhè shì wǒde dìzhǐ.
这是我的地址.

May I have your name and address?
Nín kéyǐ líugěi wǒ xìngmíng hé dìzhǐ ma?
您可以留给我姓名和地址哪?

Shall I write to you?
Wǒ géi nǐ xiěxìn hǎoma?
我给你写信好哪?

Shall we get together again? / Until next time then.
Wǒmén zài jù yícì hǎoma? / Xiàcì jiàn.
我们再聚一次好哪? / 下次见.

Socializing Tips and Tactics

Finding the Chinese (Dumping the Group)

Many people dislike group tours, but put up with them for China travel, where they offer the only practical way to tour the country with a modicum of comfort and efficiency. While avoiding the hassles with accommodations and inter-city transportation that individual travelers must face, the group tourist will have the feeling of being herded from place to place; by the third day or so, he or she will be hit with the urge to just get out on the street and stroll around. Suggestions:

Use morning and evening free time to stroll. Chinese are early risers; they're out exercising in parks and streets, or getting started with the workday long before your group will leave the hotel. They're also studying, especially English, and are looking for someone to practice on. This is a great way to get inside information on Chinese family and daily life.

Your guide or hotel staff will probably know about a local "English Corner," the name typically given to a public place where students of English gather to study and, if possible, inveigle passing Westerners into joining them in conversation. These groups generally gather in the early morning before breakfast or in the evening after dinner, just the time you might want to stroll in the park anyway. While conversations often focus on a fixed and predictable range of topics, you can guide them to your areas of interest. Also, be firm: the English practice you contribute is worth a little Chinese practice. If you strike up a friendship, make a date to meet later, perhaps the same time on another morning.

Drop out of your program occasionally. One impressive monument and breathtaking sight after another can soon become a blur, especially if you are frantically ticking them off a checksheet and missing the time to observe daily life and local color. When you are not heading for a "must-see" spot, leave the group. Be sure to tell your tour leaders, of course, so that they don't wait for you.

Arrange your own schedule. Group tours stay for the most part in modern hotels, with English-speaking staff, wake-up call services, buffet breakfasts, and available transportation, so there is no need to feel trapped (as you might have ten years ago on a China tour) by a lack of services when away from your group.

Finally, do what you want to do. If you are a typical Western tourist in China, you are probably on what amounts to the trip of a lifetime and you have paid a lot of money to get there. Go out and enjoy it.

Addressing the Chinese

This can cause some confusion. The old terms for Miss *(Xiáojie)*, Mrs. *(Fūren)*, and Mr. *(Xiānsheng)* were replaced after 1949 by the egalitarian and non-sexist Comrade *(Tóngzhi)*. However, like much revolutionary rhetoric, this has fallen out of favor. Most Chinese have gone back to the custom of addressing friends by preceding their surnames with either *Lǎo* ("Old") or *Xiǎo* ("Little"), depending upon whether they are older or younger; however, it wouldn't be appropriate for you to use these affectionate and colloquial expressions until invited to.

There are specific titles for various occupations for which a higher standard of respect is normally accorded:

Doctor	*Dàifu*	大夫
Driver	*Sijī*	司机
Manager	*Jīnglǐ*	经理
Professor	*Jiàoshòu*	教授
Teacher	*Lǎoshī*	老师
Master	*Shīfu*	师付

Note that these are placed after the surname, e.g. Wang Dàifu, "Doctor Wang." The last of these, *Shīfu*, is fairly all purpose, and can be used for any occupation which calls for some level of skill or responsibillity. Finally, if you are having trouble deciding how to address someone, just ask: *Wǒ zěnme chēnghu nǐ?* ("What should I call you?").

Other Do's and Dont's

There are *some* strictures on socialization, those that you would expect to find in a sexually and politically unliberated country. Chinese will discuss politics, especially those political subjects deemed "acceptable," e.g., horrors of the Cultural

Revolution and privileges of party big-wigs. However, it is not wise to press them on sensitive and topical issues, e.g., dissidents now on trial. Be discreet also in dealings with the opposite sex, and remember that you are burdened by some negative stereotypes that can cause your motives and actions with the opposite sex to be misinterpreted. A Western woman may be assumed by Chinese to be sexually loose; a Western man may be assumed by Chinese to be looking for a prostitute.

Because of these assumptions, it is wise to be demure in your public expressions of affection. Although China today is far less prudish than in the past, kissing and holding hands is frowned upon, and will only call attention of an unfavorable kind to a Western-Chinese couple. On the other hand, children and teenage pals of the same sex hang onto each other a great deal, a component of Asian body language that is often misinterpreted.

Friendships with Chinese may also lead to requests for favors, anything from goods that they may have difficulty getting to recommendation letters to schools and organizations abroad. These requests you will have to evaluate on an individual basis. If you feel too put upon, don't comply; on the other hand, an exchange of favors, and thus obligations, is the cement of Oriental relationships. Remember that you have much that Chinese aspire to, including the means and freedom to travel; it is not odd that they would have more requests of you than you of them.

Getting Fed

China's Culinary Regions

As might be expected of a country with a wide range of environments and ancient culinary traditions, the cuisine of China is wonderfully varied and and complex. The Chinese categorize their dishes according to four regional styles:

North (p. 120). Northern, or Mandarin, cooking has been heavily influenced by the imperial court, located in Beijing on and off for six centuries. It thus includes such exotic dishes as bird's nest soup and fish lips, as well as many of the premier dishes of China, such as Peking duck. Another strong influence has been the dishes of northern nomadic peoples, sliced meat and vegetables cooked in a single pot or on a grill, sometimes skewered. From these come Mongolian hot pot, barbecue, and kebabs. The grain staple of the north is wheat, as opposed to the rice of the south, so noodles, steamed breads, and dumplings are hearty and filling menu additions.

South (p. 121). Southern cooking, sometimes called Cantonese or Chauzhou, refers to the seemingly infinite variety of stir-fried and steamed dishes that Westerners are familiar with due to their introduction by adventurous Cantonese emigrating abroad. Southeast China is lush and fertile, producing rice and fish, and a wide variety of fruits and vegetables throughout the year.

Cantonese have a reputation for eating most anything that walks, crawls, swims, or flies—if you've been hankering for monkey, snake, or rat meat, this is the place to go—but Cantonese are gourmets as well as omnivores. Cantonese seafood is amazingly fresh and light, and this southern cooking tradition has also contributed much of the great brunch fare known as *dim sum*.

East (p. 122). Eastern cooking refers not only to Shanghaiese, but the dishes of the West Lake region and the coastal provinces of Fujian and Jiangsu, a region that has historically vied with the south for the reputation of producing the most skilled and creative chefs. Farmlands watered by the eastward-flowing Yangtze river are supposed to produce the fattest and most succulent pigs and ducks, while the river and many lakes provide freshwater shrimp, eel, crab, and carp. The soy sauce of the region is also famous and is used in braising and stir frying meats, producing dishes referred to as *hóng shǎo*, or "red cooked."

West (p. 123). Western food in China refers mainly to Sichuanese, but includes the dishes of Hunan and Yunan as well. The capital of Sichuan, Chengdu, sits in a well-watered, fertile basin with a moderate climate; historically isolated from China proper, it has nonetheless been self-sufficient in foodstuffs, and has developed a distinctly regional style. Most common and familiar are the hot dishes fired by the dried, red Sichuan pepper, and the many spicy pastes and oils in which it is a chief ingredient.

Ordering in Restaurants

Experience with actual restaurant menus will attest to fact that this four-part division is overly neat. In fact, many of China's most popular dishes can be ordered in most major restaurants. For this reason, following the lists of Chinese dishes of the four regions, additional lists are given by main ingredient. If you cannot get the exact special dish you want, at least you can get something with main ingredients that appeal to your palate.

If you are traveling with a group, your meal arrangements will generally be made for you; however, this is not necessarily an ideal situation. Groups are typically fed family style, with a variety of dishes (chicken, pork, vegetables) and soup and rice appearing in any order, or even at the same time. Although the fare is typically satisfying, you will often find a number of the same dishes appearing at the next meal, giving the impression of monotony even in the midst of abundance. Moreover, convinced that Westerners assume all Chinese food to be rice based, Chinese seldom offer groups the delicious dumplings and noodles that may be available. If you are truly interested in sampling what China's cuisine has to offer, you will have to take some control over your eating program (or turn control over to someone who shares your goals). For tips on how to do this, see "Eating Well in China," p. 136.

Of course, if you are on your own in China, you have no choice but to make your own arrangements. When eating alone it is easiest to order a single dish over rice (p. 131) or a noodle dish (p. 130). If you get a group together (a minimum of four are recommended, ten maximum), you may either order banquet style, agreeing on a per-head price for fixed menu, or order individually. If you do not have strong preferences, set banquet menus are usually a good way to go, offering a balanced variety of dishes at several price levels. Moreover, they may include local specialities that you are unaware of. Drinks will usually be extra, although often a first serving of beer or soft drink is free. You should expect and get good and plentiful food, and should not be reluctant to politely insist upon what you want; remember, your hosts want your business, and may be charging you more than a group of locals for the same meal. No tipping is necessary in restaurants. If you elect to order dishes individually, it is still best to settle on the total for the whole group in advance; in the course of deliberating you may have agreed to some delicacies that cost a good deal more than you were prepared to pay. The oily gristle touted as bear paw is an item I recall paying a premium for; I cannot recommend it.

If you are interested in sampling China's better culinary offerings, you should do as much research as possible. Ask at your hotel about local specialities, popular restaurants, and night markets.

What's the best restaurant around here?
Fùjìn zuìhǎode fàndiàn shì nǐege?
附近最好的饭店是哪个？

Is it expensive?
Guì bú guì?
贵不贵？

Could you write down the name and address?
Qíng bǎ diànmíng hé dìzhǐ xiěyíxià, hǎoma?
请把店名和地址写一下，好吗？

What are some famous local dishes?
Zhàr nǎxiē cài zuì yǒumíng?
这儿哪些菜最有名？

Could you write them down?
Géi wǒ xiěyíxià, hǎoma?
给我写一下，好吗？

I'd like an inexpensive restaurant.
Wó xiǎngqù yìjiā bú tàiguìde fàndiàn.
我想去一家不太贵的饭店．

Is there a night market nearby?
Fùjìn yǒu yèshì ma?
附近有夜市吗？

Is there any place I can have Western food?
Shénme dìfāng yǒu Xīcān?
什么地方有西餐？

Arranging a meal for a group is best done from your hotel, imposing on the concierge to help you fix the menu and book transportation.

What's the best place for **seafood**?
*Shénme dìfāngde **hǎixiān** zuìhǎo?*
什么地方的海鲜最好？

Peking duck	*Běijīng kǎoyā*	北京烤鸦
noodles	*miàntiáo*	面条
dim sum	*diǎnxīn*	点心

I'd like to arrange a meal for **four** (Numbers, p. 22)
*Wǒ xiánggěi **sìgè** rén zhǔnbèi yìcān.*
我想给四个人准备一餐．

I'd like to order **breakfast**.
*Wó xiǎng jiào **zǎofàn**.*
我想叫早饭．

lunch	*wǔfàn*	午饭
dinner	*wǎnfàn*	晚饭

I'd like to spend **50 yuan** per person. (Money, p. 28)
*Wǒ zhǔnbèi měigè rén huā **wǔshí yuán**.*
我准备每个人花五十元．

How much will it be for the entire group?
Zhéngzǔrén gòngxūyào duōshǎo qián?
整组人共需要多少钱？

Can you arrange transportation?
Nín néngfǒu ānpái jiāotōng gōngjù?
您能否安排交通工具？

When's the latest we can be served?
Zuìwǎn shénme shíhòu ānpái wǒmén?
最晚什么时候安排我们？

Breakfast is usually served from 6 to 9 and lunch from 12 to 2. Chinese eat dinner early; many restaurants stop serving around 8:30 p.m.

We have a reservation for **7:00 p.m.** (Time, p. 39)
Wǒmén yùyuē zài qīdiǎn.
我们预约在七点.

We have a reservation for **eight**. (Numbers, p. 22)
Wǒmén dìngle bāge rén de wèizi.
我们定串八个人的位子.

Do you have a table for us?
Nǐmén yǒu kòngzhuō ma?
你们有空桌吗?

Do you have a table for six?
Nǐmén yǒu méi yǒu liùrénfèn zhuōzǐ?
你们有没有六人份桌子?

We'd like a table in the **corner**.
Wǒmén xiǎngyào wūjiǎo chù yìzhāng zhuōzi.
我们想要屋角处一张桌子.

> in a no-smoking area
> *zài bù xīyān chù*
> 在不吸烟处

> in a private room
> *zài dān jiān*
> 在单间

Most large restaurants have a special section for foreigners, where the service is better and the facilities cleaner. However, you are not prohibited from eating with the public.

Excuse me!　　　(As when summoning a waiter)
Láojià!
劳驾！(or *Shīfu!* 师付！)

Does anyone speak English?
Yǒu huìshōu Yīngwénde ma?
有会说英文的吗？

May we see a menu?
Gěi wǒmén càidān kànkàn hǎoma?
给我们菜单看看好吗？

Do you have an English menu?
Yǒu méi yǒu Yīngwén càidān?
有没有英文菜单？

Do you have a set menu?
Nǐmén yǒu tàocān ma?
你们有套餐吗？

How much is it per person?
Měirén duōshǎo qián?
每人多少钱？

How many dishes does that include?
Gòng yóu jǐdào cài?
共有几道菜？

Chinese tend to eat with noise and gusto, with good sense dictating good manners. Since food is shared from a common platter, it would obviously not be polite to sift through it in search of choice morsels. Food picked up from the serving platter should be placed on a small plate or in your rice bowl before being eaten.

Are drinks included?
Yǐnliào bāokuò zài nèilema?
饮料包括在内了吗?

We want to spend a little less.
Wǒmén xiǎngyào zài piányìdiǎnde.
我们想要再便宜点的.

We could spend a little more.
Wǒmén kéyǐ yào zài guìdiǎnde.
我们可以要再贵点的.

We'd like to spend **30 yuan** each.   (Money, p. 28)
Wǒmén xiǎng měigèrén huā sānshí yuán.
我们想每个人花三十元.

Are there any local specialities?
Yǒu jù dìfāng fēngwèide cài ma?
有具地方风味的菜吗?

We'd like to try some local dishes.
Wǒmén xiǎngchī xiē yǒu dìfāng fēngwèide cài.
我们想吃些有地方风味的菜.

If you are being entertained, it is not polite to start on a new dish until bidden or served by your host. You should try at least a little of every dish, and if you can clean your plate, you will probably be served more. You should also refrain from drinking until a toast is proposed (p. 135), and should at some point propose a toast in return.

I'm **hungry**.
Wǒ èle.
我饿子.

full	*bǎole*	饱了
thirsty	*kěle*	渴
sorry	*duìbuqǐ*	对不起

We'd like a **large dish** of this.
*Zhèige wǒmén xiǎngyào **yídà pán**.*
这个我们想要一大盘.

small dish	*xiǎo pán*	小盘
medium dish	*zhōng pán*	中盘

How much altogether?
Yígòng duōshǎo qián?
一共多少钱?

May I have the check?
Qǐng bǎ zhàngdān géi wǒ hǎoma?
请把账单给我好吗?

What time do you close?
Nǐmén jídiǎn guānmén?
你们几点关门?

Some restaurants do not have table service; you purchase tickets for the items you want and take them to a counter. Look around and see what the other diners are doing.

Do you have individual rice dishes?
Nǐmén yǒu méi yǒu dāngède fànwǎn?
你们有没有单个的饭碗.

I'd like a dish with **pork**.
Wǒ xiǎngyào ge zhūròu cài.
我想要个猪肉菜.

seafood	*hǎixiān*	海鲜
chicken	*jī*	鸡
duck	*yā*	鸭
beef	*níuròu*	牛肉
lamb	*yángròu*	羊肉
tofu	*dòufu*	豆腐
vegetables	*shūcài*	蔬菜

I'd like some **rice**.
Qǐng géi wǒ lái diǎn mǐfàn.
请给我来点米饭.

water	*shuǐ*	水
soy sauce	*jiàngyóu*	酱油
chili sauce	*làjiàng*	辣酱
vinegar	*cù*	醋
sesame seed oil	*xiāngyóu*	香油
sugar	*táng*	糖
salt	*yán*	盐
pepper	*hújiāofěn*	胡椒粉

If you plan to be in China for some time, it's best to learn how to use chopsticks. Restaurants used to catering to foreigners will have knives and forks, but other will not.

I'm a vegetarian.
Wǒ chī sù.
我吃素.

I can't eat **meat**.
*Wǒ bù néng chī **ròu**.*
我不能吃肉.

pork	*zhūròu*	猪肉
dairy products	*nǎizhìpǐn*	奶制品
shellfish	*jièkéyú*	介壳鱼
MSG	*wèijīng*	味精
spicy foods	*làwèi shípǐn*	辣味食品
garlic	*dàsuàn*	大蒜
peppers	*làjiāo*	辣椒

I'd like **chopsticks**.
*Wǒ xiǎngyòng **kuàizi**.*
我想用筷子.

fork	*chāzi*	叉子
spoon	*sháozi*	勺子
soup spoon	*tāngsháo*	汤勺
napkin	*cānjīn*	餐巾
cup	*bēizi*	杯子
bowl	*wǎn*	碗
plate	*pánzi*	盘子

In Beijing, treat yourself to a Peking duck dinner or the "performance" of a Mongolian barbecue, where the chef cooks the meats and vegetables you have chosen on a huge hot griddle.

We'd like to have **Peking duck**.
*Wǒmén xiǎngyào **Běijīng kǎoyā***.
我们想要北京烤鸭.

Mongolian hot pot	*shuàn yángròu*	
	涮羊肉	
Mongolian barbeque	*Měnggǔ kǎoròu*	
	蒙古烤肉	
lamb shish kebabs	*kǎo yángròu*	
	烤羊肉	
bird's nest soup	*quêcháo tāng*	
	雀巢汤	
sweet-and-sour carp	*tángcù lǐyú*	
	糖醋鲤鱼	
fried Mandarin fish	*yúxiāng cuìpí guìyú*	
	鱼香脆皮鳜鱼	
smoked duck	*zhāngchá yāzi*	
	樟茶鸭子	
Peking pickled cabbage	*Běijīng pàocài*	
	北京泡菜	
cabbage in cream sauce	*nǎiyóu jīnbazi*	
	奶油津白子	
Shandong chicken	*cuìpí Shāndōng jī*	
	脆皮山东鸡	
cold spicy noodles	*zhá jiàng miàn*	
	炸酱面	
sweet-and-sour potato	*cùliū tǔdòu sī*	
	醋溜土豆丝	

Southern stir-fried dishes will probably appear most familiar to visitors. Seafood lovers should be sure to order some type of steamed whole fish, which is served perfectly fresh and succulent.

We'd like to have **winter melon soup**.
Wǒmén xiǎngyào dōngguā tāng.
我们想要冬瓜汤.

Cantonese fried rice	*Guǎngdōng chǎofàn*	
	广东炒饭	
steamed fish	*qīngzhēng yú*	
	清蒸鱼	
crab in black bean sauce	*dòuchǐ xiè*	
	豆豉蟹	
shrimp with mushrooms	*cǎogū xiā*	
	草菇虾	
dry-fried prawns	*zhá xiā*	
	炸虾	
asparagus with crab meat	*xièròu lúxǔn*	
	蟹肉芦笋	
Hainan chicken rice	*Hǎinán jīròu mǐfàn*	
	海南鸡肉米饭	
fried chili crab	*làjiāo chǎoxiè*	
	辣椒炒蟹	
garlic steamed mussels	*suànróng zhēng bèi*	
	蒜蓉蒸贝	
beancurd vegetables	*dòufu báicài*	
	豆腐白菜	
barbecued pork loin	*chāshāo ròu*	
	叉烧肉	
Cantonese roast duck	*Yuèshì kǎoyā*	
	越式烤鸦	

Eastern food includes a broad range of ingredients and styles, from as far south as Xiamen, across the strait from Taiwan, and reaching north to the Yellow River.

We'd like some **pan-fried chicken buns**.
*Wǒmén xiǎngyào **jīròu tēngjiǎo**.*
我们想要鸡肉樋饺.

"lion's head" meatballs	*shīzǐ tóu*
	狮子头
Xiamen fried noodles	*Xiàmén chǎomiàn xiàn*
	厦门炒面线
beggar's chicken	*qǐgài jī*
	乞丐鸡
egg slices in soup	*fúyáng dàntāng*
	芙阳蛋汤
Yangchow fried rice	*Yángzhōu chǎofàn*
	杨州炒饭
Shanghai smoked fish	*Shànghǎi kǎoyú*
	上海烤鱼
Shanghai cabbage rice	*Shànghǎi càifàn*
	上海菜饭
"eight-treasures" beancurd	*bābǎo dòufu*
	八宝豆腐
poached West Lake fish	*Xīhú cùyú*
	西湖脆鱼
steamed pork buns	*xiǎolóng bāo*
	小笼包
Shanghai fried noodles	*Shànghǎi chǎomiàn*
	上海炒面
Shanghai greens	*Shànghǎi qīngcài*
	上海青菜

If you like hot and spicy food, you will enjoy the foods of Hunan, Yunan, and Sichuan. Sichuan also boasts a *dim sum* menu with some livelier dishes than their Cantonese counterparts.

We'd like to have **spicy beancurd with pork**.
*Wǒmén xiǎngyào **mápó dòufu**.*
我们想要麻婆豆腐.

spicy egg noodles	*dàndàn miàn*
	担担面
"cross-the-bridge" noodles	*guòqiáo miàn*
	过桥面
prawns in chili	*yúxiāng dàxiā*
	鱼香大虾
"twice-cooked" pork	*húiguō ròu*
	回锅肉
"home-style" beef	*jiācháng niúròusī*
	家常牛肉丝
"ants climbing trees"	*máyǐ shàngshù*
	蚂蚁上树
cold Chengdu noodles	*Chéngdū lěngmiàn*
	成都冷面
spicy eggplant	*yúxiāng qiézǐ*
	鱼香茄子
dry-fried beans	*gānbiàn sìjìdòu*
	干扁四季豆
fragrant crispy duck	*cuìpí yā*
	脆皮鸦
chicken with peppers	*gōngbǎo jīdīng*
	宫保鸡丁
Hunan shrimp and pork	*Húnán liǎng yàng*
	湖南两样

Pork is the meat staple of China and a pork dish will be part of every meal. Beef is less important in the Chinese diet, as cattle (oxen) were raised chiefly for work, not as a food source. Lamb dishes are common in northern and far western China, where nomads tend flocks of sheep.

We'd like to have **pork and Chinese pickles**.
*Wǒmén xiǎngyào **zhàcài ròusī**.*
我们想要榨菜肉丝.

sweet-and-sour pork	*tiánsuān ròu*	甜酸肉 .
pork with garlic sauce	*suànní báiròu*	蒜泥白肉
meatballs and spinach	*dōngpō xiùqiú*	东波秀球
fried pork and beancurd	*dòufǔ ròujiāng zhá*	豆腐肉酱炸
spareribs in bean sauce	*dòuchǐ páigǔ*	豆豉排骨
beef with sesame seeds	*zhīmá niúpái*	芝麻牛排
soy-braised beef	*hóngshāo niúròu*	红烧牛肉
beef with green peppers	*qīngjiāo niúròu sī*	青椒牛肉丝
lamb with scallions	*cōngbào yángròu*	葱爆羊肉
lamb in sweet bean sauce	*jiàng yángròu*	酱羊肉
lamb with dipping sauce	*zhá yángpái*	炸羊排

After pork, chicken is the most ubiquitous meat on the Chinese table. The flesh of feathered creatures has been traditionally regarded as healthier than other meats and has figured prominently in medicinal preparations.

We'd like **steamed chicken with scallions**.
*Wŏmén xiǎngyào **qīngzhēng jī**.*
我们想要清蒸鸡.

Hunan smoked chicken	*Húnán xūnjī*	湖南熏鸡
soy-braised chicken	*hóngshāo jī*	红烧鸡
chicken with cashews	*yāoguǒ jī*	腰果鸡
"eight treasures" chicken	*bābǎo jī*	八宝鸡
sweet-and-sour livers	*tiánsuān jīgān*	甜酸鸡肝
lemon chicken	*níngméng jī*	柠檬鸡
sesame chicken	*zhīmá jī*	芝麻鸡
chicken curry	*jiālǐ jīpiàn*	咖喱鸡片
chicken with spinach	*bōcài jīsī*	菠菜鸡丝
chicken with walnuts	*hétáo jīdīng*	核桃鸡丁
duck with oranges	*chénpí zhēngyā*	陈皮蒸鸭
crispy skin duck	*xiāngsū yā*	香酥鸭

Although pond-raised carp prepared in a multitude of ways is the staple fish of China, seafood offerings range from the lowly *bêche-de-mer* ("sea slugs" to those who don't favor them) to Shanghai hairy crabs, an expensive seasonal delicacy.

We'd like a **deep-fried sweet and sour carp**.
Wǒmén xiǎngyào tángcù lǐyú.
我们想要糖醋鲤鱼.

fish in spicy sauce	*dòubànjiàng yú* 豆瓣酱鱼
soy-braised yellow fish	*hóngshāo huángyú* 红烧黄鱼
crispy shrimp with garlic	*yánsū xiā* 咸酥虾
chili pepper shrimp	*làwèi xiā* 辣味虾
shrimp and eggs	*fúróng xiā* 芙蓉虾
squid with bamboo	*sǔnsī yóuyú juǎn* 笋丝鱿鱼卷
crispy squid	*sūzhá yóuyú* 酥茶鱿鱼
ginger and scallion crab	*cōngbào pángxiè* 葱爆螃蟹
crab in sweet bean sauce	*jīngjiàng xièròu* 京酱蟹肉
scallops in oyster sauce	*háoyóu xiānbèi* 蚝油鲜贝
scallops with broccoli	*jièlán xiānbèi* 芥蓝鲜贝

In addition to the many vegetables and beancurd dishes on ordinary restaurant menus, China's ancient Buddhist beliefs have given rise to a rich and varied vegetarian cuisine. Vegetarian restaurants feature "mock" meat and seafood dishes, actually prepared entirely from vegetable ingredients.

We'd like the **vegetarian prawns**.
*Wǒmén xiǎngyào **lóhàn dàxiā**.*
我们想要罗汉大虾.

"shrimp" balls	*sù zhá wánzǐ*
	素炸丸子
lion's head "meatballs"	*sù shīzǐtóu*
	素狮子头
sweet and sour "pork"	*sù tángcù ròu*
	素糖醋肉
broccoli in "crabmeat"	*sù xiè jièlán*
	素蟹界蓝
vegetarian fried rice	*sù chǎofàn*
	素炒饭
stir-fried greens	*chǎo qīngcài*
	炒青菜
vegetables in beancurd	*shūcài dòufǔ*
	蔬菜豆腐
beancurd soup	*dòufǔ tāng*
	豆腐汤
vegetarian noodles in soup	*sùcài miàntāng*
	素菜面汤
vegetarian spring rolls	*sù chūnjuǎn*
	素春卷
mixed vegetables	*sù shí jǐn*
	素什锦

Chinese soups consist of both palate-cleansing broths and hearty main-course soups. In a Chinese banquet, soups may appear at any time between courses.

We'd like **hot-and-sour soup**.
Wǒmén xiǎngyào **suān là tāng**.
我们想要酸辣汤.

vegetable beancurd soup	*shūcài dòufu tāng* 蔬菜豆腐汤	
wonton soup	*yúntún tāng* 云吞汤	
seafood hot pot	*wǔfú hǎixiān huǒguō* 五福海鲜火锅	
egg-drop soup	*dànhuā tāng* 蛋花汤	
vegetable beef soup	*niúròu càitāng* 牛肉菜汤	
crabmeat and corn soup	*xièròu yùmǐ tāng* 蟹肉玉米汤	
vegetable chowder	*yuántāng sùhùi* 原汤素烩	
duck and noodle soup	*báicài yātāng* 白菜鸭汤	
clear oxtail soup	*niúwěi tāng* 牛尾汤	
pork and pickle soup	*zhàcài ròusī tāng* 榨菜肉丝汤	
chicken and pickle soup	*huáng guā dùnjī* 黄瓜炖鸡	
spinach meatball soup	*bōcài ròuwán tāng* 菠菜肉丸汤	

A typical Chinese breakfast is *xīfàn* or *dàmǐ zhōu*, a rice porridge that is livened up with toppings such as scrambled egg, bits of pork, peanuts, pickles, etc. An alternate menu is a fried cruller or sesame pancake, with or without sweet soybean soup called *dòujiāng*. Tourists in groups will most always be served the Chinese interpretation of a Western breakfast. By all means try some Chinese desserts, although Westerners often find them overly sweet. See p. 134 for drinks.

We'd like some **rice porridge**.
*Wǒmén xiǎngyào **dàmǐ zhōu**.*
我们想要大米粥.

fried cruller	*yóutiáo*	油条
sesame pancake	*zhīmá bǐng*	芝麻饼
soybean soup	*dòujiāng*	豆浆
fried eggs	*zhá jīdàn*	炸鸡蛋
scrambled eggs	*chǎo jīdàn*	炒鸡蛋
hard-boiled eggs	*zhǔ jīdàn*	煮鸡蛋
toast	*miànbāo*	面饱
jam	*guǒjiàng*	果酱
butter	*nǎiyóu*	奶油
almond cookies	*xìngrén bǐng*	杏仁饼
walnut cookies	*hétáo bǐng*	核桃饼
mango pudding	*mángguǒ bùdīng*	芒果布丁
red bean soup	*dòushā zhōu*	豆沙粥
rice dumplings	*zòngzǐ*	粽子
moon cakes	*yuèbǐng*	月饼
custard tarts	*dàntǎ*	蛋塔

The Chinese supposedly invented pasta, which was then brought to Italy by Marco Polo. Look for noodles being made fresh, which should insure a delicious meal.

We'd like **fried noodles with pork**.
*Wǒmén xiǎngyào **ròusī chǎomiàn**.*
我们想要肉丝炒面.

shrimp fried noodles	*xiārén chǎomiàn* 虾仁炒面	
chicken fried noodles	*jīròu chǎomiàn* 鸡肉炒面	
beef fried noodles	*niúròu chǎomiàn* 牛肉炒面	
vegetable fried noodles	*shūcài chǎomiàn* 蔬菜炒面	
plain noodles in soup	*miàntiáo* 面条	
beef noodle soup	*niúròu tāngmiàn* 牛肉汤面	
chicken noodle soup	*jīsī tāngmiàn* 鸡丝汤面	
pork noodle soup	*chāshǎo tāngmiàn* 叉烧汤面	
curried beef noodles	*gālí niúròu miàn* 咖喱牛肉面	
noodles with duck	*yāròu miàn* 鸦肉面	
pork and pickle noodles	*zhācài ròusī miàn* 榨菜肉丝面	
Singapore vermicelli	*Xīnzhōu mífěn* 新洲米粉	

The individual diner can order a *kèfàn*, an individual portion of a dish poured over white rice. And the various types of fried rice make a good meal for one. These will usually be served with tea or broth.

I'd like **shrimp fried rice**.
*Wó xiăngyào **xiārén chăofàn**.*
我想要虾仁炒饭.

chicken fried rice	*jīsī chăofàn*	
	鸡丝炒饭	
pork fried rice	*ròusī chăofàn*	
	肉丝炒饭	
vegetable fried rice	*sùcài chăofàn*	
	素菜炒饭	
mixed fried rice	*shíjǐn chăofàn*	
	什锦炒饭	
beef fried rice	*niúròusī chăofàn*	
	牛肉丝炒饭	
curried fried rice	*gālifàn*	
	咖喱饭	
shrimp with sizzling rice	*guōbā xiārén*	
	锅巴虾仁	
pork chop and rice	*páigǔ fàn*	
	排骨饭	
duck and rice	*yāròu fàn*	
	鸭肉饭	
beef and vegetable rice	*niúròu huìfàn*	
	牛肉烩饭	
shrimp and chicken rice	*bào shuāngdīng fàn*	
	爆双丁饭	
fried egg and scallion rice	*cōnghuā jīdàn fàn*	
	葱花鸡蛋饭	

Dim sum is Cantonese for *diǎn xīn,* or "little hearts," small snacks usually served from carts and consumed at a leisurely pace with tea. Don't let your lack of Chinese-language skills keep you away from a *dim sum* restaurant; here you can look and point. As you are served, a running tally of the dishes you have ordered will be kept at your table. This is your check.

I'd like some **steamed pork dumplings**.
Wó xiǎngyào shāomài.
我想要烧卖.

steamed pork buns	*chāshāo bāo* 叉烧包
fried pork dumplings	*guōtiē* 锅贴
"wonton" dumplings	*húndùn* 云吞
spring rolls	*chūnjuǎn* 春卷
stuffed peppers	*niàng qīngjiāo* 酿青椒
beef balls	*níuròu wán* 牛肉丸
spareribs	*páigǔ* 排骨
shrimp dumplings	*xīa jiǎo* 虾饺
shrimp balls	*xīa wán* 虾丸
stuffed lotus leaves	*nùomǐ jī* 糯米鸡

Night markets often have restaurants with outdoor seating serving the full range of dishes listed on the previous pages. These will also be small stands or carts serving the snacks listed below.

I'd like **fried pork dumplings**.
Wó xiǎngyào **guōtiē.**
我想要锅贴.

boiled dumplings	*shuǐjiǎo*	
	水饺	
steamed buns	*mántou*	
	馒头	
meat-stuffed buns	*ròu bāozi*	
	肉包子	
fried vermicelli	*chǎo mǐfěn*	
	炒米粉	
baked yams	*kǎo báishǔ*	
	烤白薯	
scallion pancake	*cōngyóubǐng*	
	葱油饼	
vegetable roll	*chūnjuǎn*	
	春卷	
fried chicken wings	*zhá jīchì*	
	炸鸡翅	
caramelized fruit	*shānzhā chuàn*	
	山楂串	
caramelized yams	*básì shānyào*	
	拔丝山药	
caramelized apples	*básì píngguǒ*	
	拔丝苹果	
beef jerky	*niúròu gān*	
	牛肉干	

Chinese believe ardently in the digestive and restorative benefits of tea, which is consumed without sugar, milk, or lemon. Chinese sodas are often overly sweet.

Please bring us some **green tea**.
Qǐng géi wǒmen qīngchá.
请给我们青茶.

green tea	*lǜchá*	绿茶
black tea	*hóngchá*	红茶
jasmine tea	*mòlì huāchá*	茉莉花茶
oolong tea	*wūlóng chá*	乌龙茶
chrysanthe-mum tea	*huāchá*	花茶
mineral water	*kuàngquán shuǐ*	矿泉水
boiled water	*kāi shuǐ*	开水
cold boiled water	*liáng kāi shuǐ*	凉开水
coffee	*kāfēi*	咖啡
sugar	*táng*	糖
milk	*niúnǎi*	牛奶
soy milk	*dòujiāng*	豆酱
lemonade	*níng méng shuǐ*	柠檬水
orange juice	*júzi zhī*	桔子汁
soda (pop)	*qìshuǐ*	汽水

Although most Westerners know only the popular export beer Qingdao, China has hundreds of local breweries, and beer varies widely in taste and quality. Chinese liquors are often too strange or sweet for foreign taste buds. Note that the word *jiǔ* includes both fermented and distilled products. Those indicated in quotes below ("wine") are in fact strong spirits.

I'd like a beer, please.
Wó xiǎngyào píng píjiǔ.
我想要瓶啤酒.

Do you have any cold?
Nín yǒu lěngdòngde mā?
你有冷冻的吗?

I'd like **brandy**.
Wǒ yào báilándì.
我要白兰地.

whiskey	*wéishìjì*	威士忌
grape wine	*pútáojiǔ*	葡萄酒
rice wine	*mǐjiǔ*	米酒
Guilin rice "wine"	*Guìlín mǐjiǔ*	桂林米酒
Maotai "wine"	*Máotái jiǔ*	毛苔酒
Shaoxing "wine"	*Shàoxīng jiǔ*	绍兴酒
five spices wine	*wǔliangyè*	五粮液

Bottoms up!   (Literally "Dry glass!")
Gānbēi!
干杯!

Thank you everybody.
Xièxiè gèwèi.
谢谢各位.

Eating Well in China

A Brief History of Tourist Food

Since the opening of the People's Republic to tourism, the Chinese food available to foreign tourists has undergone an odd evolution in quality. Through the early 1980s, it was uniformly poor. Unless you were a VIP staying at a government guest house, you suffered the institutional output of hotel kitchens and the few restaurants awarded CITS approval for sanitation. Vegetables and fruits were available only in season; if you traveled in North China in the spring you faced cauliflower and cabbage at every meal. At Narita and Hong Kong, standard overnight stops for groups flying back to the States, there would be a veritable citrus and salad feeding frenzy at the breakfast buffet.

Things got better. China became more prosperous and its infrastructure dramatically improved. Tourism boomed and local organizations increasingly competed with hotels in the growth industry of feeding foreigners. The competition produced some surprises: in 1984 I ate at the best Sichuan restaurant I had ever experienced *in* Sichuan, operated by the People's Liberation Army. Savvy tour group leaders would demand to have their groups taken "outside" to eat, knowing that any place arranged for them would probably be better than their hotel.

The end of the decade ushered in the era of the joint-venture hotel. Staff trainers from Europe and chefs from Hong Kong were brought in to upgrade food and service. By the early 1990s, the best restaurants in the best hotels of Beijing and Shanghai were as good as those of Hong Kong and Taipei. Then something odd happened. Returning from a hard day's sightseeing, and looking forward to a nice meal at your hotel (perhaps recalling your delightful breakfast buffet), you would suddenly be told by your guide that you would be going *out* to eat. You would then be taken to a restaurant reminiscent of 1980s China, complete with dirty tablecloths and bad service.

What happened? The joint-venture hotels simply became too expensive for the CITS, which must now turn elsewhere to get its charges fed. Nor do the best of the new local restaurants have need of the meagre CITS per-head allotment; like the hotels, they are full of Chinese happy to pay the full price for good food. The days of the lordly foreign guest getting the best of everything are over; the Chinese have money now and you must compete with them. What can you do to avoid mediocre institutional Chinese food?

Go armed with information. Consult up-to-date guidebooks and Nina Simond's *China's Food.* Note recommended restaurants in the cities you will be taken to and ask that your local Chinese guide arrange a meal there. You will probably have to pay extra but it will be a modest amount compared with food in the West and in almost all cases be worth it. (Note, however, that this may not always be possible on a tight schedule; be content with the plans for the first evening you arrive in a city but request that special arrangements be made for the following night.)

Drop out of the group. Your local guide may honestly try and be unable to arrange a dinner for a group of twenty-five at a specified restaurant. Go yourself with a smaller group, at least four, no more than ten; perhaps the same place can squeeze you in at a single table. Or perhaps your local guide never called; ask your hotel concierge to arrange dinner for you. In any case, get recommendations from the hotel staff.

Go where the Chinese go. Follow that old rule of thumb: go to the restaurants that are crowded because that's where the good food is. In China, this often means a barnlike, brightly lit, and garishly decorated hall where waiters shout across the room to be heard above the clatter of the dishes. To the Chinese, these are prerequisites for good dining; they would feel quite gloomy and ill at ease trapped in a cozy Western bistro with subdued lighting and the quiet, obsequious service we prize.

Head for the night market. Every city has night markets selling food to those out for the evening or working odd hours. Health considerations are certainly germane, but if you apply common sense you should have no problem. Eat foods that are hot; noodle soups and stir-fried dishes, prepared as you watch, are recommended. You might want to stay away (I won't) from dumplings and fried meat items that have been cooked earlier and are just sitting out there. If you wish to be extra cautious, take your own plastic bowl and chopsticks (available in any department store); vendors in most markets are used to this strange foreign fetish.

Seek out minority foods and local specialties. If you go to western China, insist on trying Muslim food, with its great breads and lamb dishes. If you go to southwest China, try the food of the Dai people, a wonderful cross between Chinese and Thai. Have a dumpling banquet in Xian and *mápó dòufu* in Chengdu. Again, consult some good guidebooks before you go so that you can request these items in case your local guides do not. Remember that your guides are practically always Han Chinese, who are unused to and may even dislike the local offerings so appealing to you.

Stay in your hotel. This will strike Old China Hands as a bizzare thing to say. But if you are staying at the Sheraton in Urumqi, or certainly the Holiday Inn in Lhasa, the best restaurants in town are right in your hotel. If the group is going out to eat, I'd ask why and think about declining if a compelling answer is not forthcoming.

Getting What You Need

Conventional wisdom has it that there is no worthwhile shopping in China. If you are seeking cutting-edge fashion at bargain prices or museum-quality antiques of documented provenance, this is true; for others, however, from merely curious window shoppers to avid bargain hunters of all stripes, China offers something that will please. The goods suggested below, ranging from the exotic to the mundane, are only a partial listing.

The government-run antique stores in most larger cities, and their subsidiaries located conveniently in tourist hotels, offer souvenirs and antiques of reliable quality and authenticity, although the items will not be grand bargains and the sellers may not come down a good deal. For more interesting old knicknacks and better prices, explore the wares at the street markets that line the main approaches to active temples; typical offerings are old locks, odd ceramic and cloisonne items, costume jewelry, woodcarvings, small jade pieces, and religious items such as Buddhist prayer beads. You should bargain, of course, and never pay a great deal for anything on the vendor's assurance of its value unless you are an expert yourself.

For carpets, cloisonne, jade carving, scroll painting, and silk and embroidery, tourists are often directed (or dragged) to the local "factory" that produces one, or all, of these treasures. These trips can be interesting, for they present an opportunity to see how these items, or at least their modern counterparts, are made. And, of course, every factory has a gift shop, which may or may not offer some respectable candidates for purchase. In spite of what you might be told, and what most guidebooks advise, you should try to bargain here.

My personal preference is for ordinary items that are used daily but that exhibit perhaps traditional design or a high degree of craftsmanship. I bought a fine bone-inlaid stringed instrument called a *heijik* in Kashgar; a copper Tibetan butter-tea pot in Xian, and a carved wooden mold for decorative cookies in Shanghai. Department stores, hardware and other specialty stores, as well as street markets and agricultural fairs are the best places to search for such items, which will not be stocked in government "Friendship Stores" because the Chinese don't realize that visitors from abroad might be interested in them.

A word about ivory: the advice from the reputable leadership of groups who care about our planet is, don't buy it. It is true that antique ivory items (over one hundred years old) can be legally imported. However, the demand on ivory of any type seems to create pressure to supply that demand through illegal sources and means. Forged certificates of origin and age are routinely offered; these will not be accepted by U.S. Customs agents. The same advice holds for exotic-animal goods of all types, especially the reptile skins and furs you will find out west and the exotic medicinal preparations you will find in traditional pharmacies (although these latter will not likely be calling out to you to buy).

Gift foods and beverages are a good way of investigating what the Chinese like and are always of interest, or at least amusing, to those back home. Many teas, dried fruits, and candies are good, and medicinal preparations (not the rhino horn!) often promise, in wonderfully fractured English, to cure what ails you. For a few dollars, who can pass up a tea that promises to "prevent and cure cancer"? Note that ordinary grocery items have been omitted here, on the assumption that most users of this book are visitors to China who will not be shopping and cooking. For snacks and street foods, see p. 133.

Finally, for those traveling to remoter regions, unusual ethnic items can always be found, including textiles, clothing, jewelry, kitchenware, and utensils. Again, these are most often found in smaller shops or in street markets where you can bargain. Especially in Tibet and western China, you will find that U.S. dollars in small denominations are the most convenient and powerful medium of exchange.

Antiques, Old and New

Although China still has strict laws on the books controlling the sale of antiquities, illegal trafficking of antiques is at present out of control. Provincial museums strapped for cash (or controlled by corrupt officials) have "de-accessioned" entire collections, the remnants of which can be viewed in the shops of Hollywood Road, the antique market area of Hong Kong. These are supplemented with truckloads of relics from all over the mainland that exit across international borders daily.

At the same time the market in replicas (or fakes, depending on buyer expectations), is flourishing. Duplicating the old is a time-honored Chinese pastime, and these guys are good. Bronzes are treated with chemicals and buried to develop the patinas of their authentic Shang and Zhou models; Han, Tang, and Ming burial figures are painstakingly recreated with appropriately contemporary glazes; Ming blue porcelains and Qing imperial yellow pieces, complete with authentic looking reign-period markings, are being turned out at the same ceramic centers, such as Jing De Zhen, that have been supplying these goods to the upper classes for centuries.

Thus *caveat emptor* is the watchword for those with more money to spend on authentic antiques than they would care to lose; the rest of us, however, can delight in this bargain basement of art replicas. The initial assertion that a piece is genuine is usually quickly abandoned. (Me: "How much?" Reply: "1,000 yuan. It's Ming." Me: "How about 100?" Reply: "OK.") In established "antique markets," however, replicas are sometimes mixed with genuine old pieces, and dealers, assuming their customers will be unable to distinguish between them, hold out for higher prices. The only sensible way to approach this madness is simply to be realistic; you are not going to get for $100 a Han dynasty burial figurine that will fetch $5,000 at Sotheby's.

A full range of specialty stores will be found only in China's largest cities, where they are usually conveniently gathered along well-known shopping streets or districts (Wang Fu Jing in Beijing; Nanjing Road in Shanghai; etc.). For sources of services (banks, post offices, barbershops, etc.), see p. 165.

Where is an **antique store**?
Gúdǒng diàn zài nǎr?
古董店在哪儿?

Friendship Store	*Yǒuyì Shāngdiàn*	友谊商店
camera shop	*zhàoxiàng qìcái shāngdiàn*	照象器材商店
hardware store	*wǔjīn shāngdiàn*	五金商店
jewelry store	*zhūbǎo shǒushì diàn*	珠宝手饰店
stationery store	*wénjù diàn*	文具店
bookstore	*shūdiàn*	书店
department store	*bǎihùo shāngdiàn*	百货商店
drug store	*yàodiàn*	药店
greengrocer	*shūcaì diàn*	蔬菜店
supermarket	*zìxǔan shāngdiàn*	自选商店
shoe shop	*xíediàn*	鞋店
optician	*yǎnjìng diàn*	眼镜店
toy store	*wánjù diàn*	玩具店
sporting goods store	*tǐyù yòngpǐn shāngdiàn*	体育用品商店

The following expressions will be useful in any shop or market. You may also wish to review the terms for expresing amounts of money (p. 28).

Excuse me!
Duìbuqǐ!
对不起!

Can you help me?
Nǐ néng bāngbāng wǒ ma?
你能帮帮我吗?

I'd like to buy one of those.
Wǒ xiángmǎi nèige.
我想买那个.

I'm just looking.
Wǒ xiān kànkan.
我先看看.

How much is this?
Zhèige duōshǎo qián?
这个多少钱?

That's quite expensive.
Nà hěn guì.
那很贵.

Can you make it a little cheaper?
Piányìdiǎn, xíngma?
便宜点, 行吗?

Conventional wisdom holds that if you see something you want, buy it, because you probably won't find it again. Choices available to consumers in China are often limited and stocks erratic. However, it never hurts to ask.

Please show me some others.
Qǐng zài ná jǐge géi wǒ kànkan.
请再拿几个给我看看.

Do you have a **bigger** one?
*Yǒu **dà yìdiǎn** de ma?*
有大一点的吗?

smaller	*xiǎo yìdiǎn*	小一点
cheaper	*piányìdiǎn*	便宜点
lighter	*qīng diǎn*	轻点
heavier	*zhòng diǎn*	重点
brighter	*liàng diǎn*	亮点
darker	*hēi diǎn*	黑点
better	*háo diǎn*	好点
sturdier	*jiēshí diǎn*	结实点

I'll take this one.
Wǒ juédìng mǎi zhège.
我决定买这个.

It's not quite what I want.
Zhège bútài líxiǎng.
这个不太理想.

Remember that in China and most of Asia, black is formal, but white is associated with death. Red is an auspicious color, and you will see plenty of it.

Do you have other colors?
Biéde yánsè yǒu méi yǒu?
别的颜色有没有？

Do you have it in **white**?
*Zhège yǒu **báisè** de ma?*
这个有白色的吗？

black	*hēisè*	黑色
red	*hóngsè*	红色
orange	*chénghuángsè*	橙黄色
yellow	*huángsè*	黄色
green	*lǜsè*	绿色
blue violet	*zǐluólánsè*	紫罗兰色
brown	*zōngsè*	棕色
gray	*huīsè*	灰色

Can I use a credit card?
Wǒ yòng xìnyòng kǎ, xíng ma?
我用信用卡，行吗？

Where can I change money?
Wǒ zài nǎr duìhuàn chāopiào?
我在哪儿兑换钞票？

Please give me a receipt.
Qǐng kāi zhāng shōujù.
请开张收据.

Antiques in China that can be legally exported
are marked with a wax seal. However, this seal
does not authenticate any age or provenance, as is
sometimes asserted. Ask for a receipt, especially
for objects that appear genuinely old but lack the
required seal, although one will not be forthcoming at a local outdoor market. See also "Antiques,
Old and New," p. 143.

Where can I buy antiques?
Zài nǎr néng mǎi gúdǒng?
在哪儿能买古董？

How old is it?
Nǎge niándàide?
哪个年代的？

From which dynasty?
Něige cháodàide?
哪个朝代的？

I'd like to buy some **old coins**?
Wǒ xiǎngmǎi gǔbì.
我想买古币.

bronze pieces	*qīngtóng zhìpǐn*	青铜制品
calligraphy	*shūfǎ*	书法
carpets	*dìtǎn*	地毯
carved objects	*diāokè pǐn*	雕刻品
ceramics	*táocí*	陶瓷
clocks	*zhōng*	钟
cloisonne ware	*jǐngtàilán*	景泰蓝
dolls	*wáwa*	娃娃

f you search avidly, you will certainly find some
nteresting pieces outside of government stores,
perhaps even something genuinely valuable; the
owners, after all, are confident that they can get
more from you than from the government. Certainly purchase nothing of greater value than you
would care to risk losing at customs. See also
"Jewelry," p. 159.

Do you have any **embroidery**?
***Xiùhuā zhìpǐn** yǒu ma?*
秀花制品有吗？

fans	*shànzi*	扇子
folding screens	*zhédié píngfēng*	折叠屏风
jade pieces	*yùshí zhìpǐn*	玉石制品
jewelry	*shǒushì*	手饰
lacquerware	*qīqì*	漆器
musical instruments	*yuèqì*	乐器
paper cuts	*jiánzhǐ*	剪纸
paintings	*huà*	画
pearls	*zhēnzhū*	珍珠
porcelain	*cíqì*	瓷器
scrolls	*juànzhóu*	卷轴
snuff bottles	*bíyānhú*	鼻烟壶
silks	*sīzhīpǐn*	丝织品
stone rubbings	*shímó*	石磨

In addition to the Western stationery items you require, you may wish to look at Chinese scholars' implements; these include writing brushes and brush pots, inksticks and inkstones, brush rests, paperweights, and meditative "scholar's stones." All are quite handsome and make excellent souvenirs.

I'd like to buy some **pencils**.
Wǒ xiángmǎi **qiānbǐ.**
我想买铅笔.

pens	*gāngbǐ*	钢笔
erasers	*xiàngpí*	橡皮
stationery	*wénjù*	文具
envelopes	*xìnfēng*	信封
air letters	*hángkōng xìn*	航空信
airmail stationery	*hángkōng wénjù*	航空文具
postcards	*míngxìnpiàn*	明信片
wrapping paper	*bāozhuāng yòngzhǐ*	包装用纸
calligraphy brushes	*máobǐ*	毛笔
ink sticks	*mò*	墨
inkstones	*mòpán*	墨盘
brush pots	*bǐtǒng*	笔筒

Tourist hotels will have the best selection of Western books and magazines. The New China Bookstore, *Xīnhúa Shūdìan*, with branches in most cities, has the largest selection of English-language materials printed in China. These typically include local and provincial maps, cheap and good bilingual dictionaries, and full-color, "beautiful China" books on the nation and the region.

Do you have **English-language newspapers**?
Yīngwén bàozhǐ yǒu ma?
英文报纸有吗？

books in English	*Yīngyǔshū*
	英语书
maps in English	*Yīngwén dìtú*
	英文地图
Chinese-English dictionaries	*Hàn-Yīng cídiǎn*
	汉英词典
English-Chinese dictionaries	*Yīng-Hàn cídiǎn*
	英汉词典
Chinese phrasebooks	*Zhōngwén cízǔ shǒucè*
	中文词组手册
books for studying Chinese	*xué Zhōngwén shǒucè*
	学中文手册
tapes for studying Chinese	*xué Zhōngwén cídài*
	学中文磁带
guidebooks	*zhǐnán*
	指南
a map of the city	*shìqūtú*
	市区图
a map of China	*Zhōngguó dìtú*
	中国地图

Chinese use mostly standard 100 ASA color print film. If you shoot any other type you should take an adequate supply with you when away from the bigger cities. For film processing and other photographic services, see p. 176.

Do you have a **35-mm camera**?
Yǒu méi yǒu sānshíwǔ-háomǐ jìngtóu zhàoxiàngjī?
有没有三十五毫米镜头照象机？

disposable camera	*yícìxìng zhàoxiàngjī*	一次性照象机
zoom lens	*kěbiàn jiāojù jìngtóu*	可变焦距镜头
wide-angle lens	*guǎngjiāo jìngtóu*	广焦镜头
telephoto lens	*wàngyuǎn jìngtóu*	望远镜头
battery	*diànchí*	电池
carrying case	*wàitào*	外套
light meter	*bàoguāng biǎo*	曝光表
tripod	*sānjiǎo jià*	三角架
color print film	*cǎisè jiāo juǎn*	彩色胶卷
color slide film	*cǎisè huàn dēng piàn*	彩色幻灯片
black and white film	*hēibái jiāo juǎn*	黑白胶卷
24 exposures	*èrshísì zhāngde*	二十四张的
36 exposures	*sānshíliù zhāngde*	三十六张的
64 ASA	*lìushísì ASA*	六十四 ASA
400 ASA	*sìbǎi ASA*	四百 ASA

China is accused of rampant piracy of Western intellectual property, including audio products. The impact of this practice is grossly overstated (figures are cited based on loss of sales of the comparable genuine product, as if the average Chinese would or could fork out the equivalent of $15 for a favorite gangsta' rapper), but besides that, the temptingly low-priced pirated products you will see are of very poor quality. However, since tapes are very cheap in China, take home a selection of traditional and ethnic music.

Do you have some Chinese popular music?
Yǒu méi yǒu Zhōngguó liúxíng yīnyuè.
有没有中国流行音乐？

Could you recommend some **traditional music?**
*Qǐng géiwǒ jièshào yìxiē **chuántǒng yīnyuè**, hǎoma?*
请给我介绍一些传统音乐，好吗？

music of minority peoples	*shǎoshù mínzú yīnyuè*	少数民族音乐
instrumentals	*yuèqì*	乐器
Beijing opera	*Jīngjù*	京剧
Cantonese opera	*Yuèjù*	越剧
folk music	*dìfāng yīnyuè*	地方音乐

Does this come in a CD?
Zhèi yǒu méi yǒu jīguāng chàngpán?
这有没有激光唱盘？

Does this come in a cassette?
Zhèi yǒu méi yǒu cídài?
这有没有磁带？

Chinese electrical current is 220 volts, 50 cycles. Thus your choice with electrical appliances is either to make due with the appliances you have brought from home, using the necessary adapters, or buy something inexpensive to use in China.

Do you have a voltage adapter for this?
Nín yǒu méi yǒu biànyāqì?
您有没有变压器？

I want to use this in China.
Wǒ xiǎng zài Zhōngguó yòng.
我想在中国用.

Can I use this in the U.S.?
Zhèige néng zài Měiguó yòng ma?
这个能在美国用吗？

Do you have a battery for this?
Nín yǒu méi yǒu pèi zhèigede diànchí?
您有没有配这个的电池？

Can you fix this?
Nín néng fǒ xiūlǐ zhèige?
您能否修理这个？

I'd like to buy a **portable radio**?
*Wǒ xiǎngmǎi ge **shǒutí shōuyīnjī**.*
我想买个手提收音机.

short wave radio	*duǎnpō shōuyīnjī*	短波收音机
extension cord	*zhuǎnjiē diànxiàn*	转接电线
electric razor	*diàndòng tìxūdāo*	电动剃须刀
hair dryer	*hōngfàjī*	烘发机
lamp	*dēng*	灯

Hardware stores are a good place to see the tools that average Chinese use for the tasks of daily life, as well as find items useful for travel in China. This is where you will find a sturdy thermos to take on the train, or those tiny luggage locks that Chinese demand on checked baggage. There are also hardware sections in department stores.

I'd like to buy a **thermos bottle**.
*Wǒ xiángmǎi ge **nuǎn shuǐpíng***.
我想买个暖水瓶.

canteen	*shuǐhú*	水壶
thermos	*rèshuǐpíng*	热水瓶
fruit peeler	*qùpídāo*	去皮刀
pocket knife	*xiǎodāo*	小刀
bottle opener	*kāi píngdāo*	开瓶刀
can opener	*kāi guàntóu dāo*	开罐头刀
corkscrew	*píngsāizuàn*	瓶塞钻
flashlight	*shǒudiàn*	手电
scissors	*jiǎndāo*	剪刀
screw driver	*xuánzáo*	旋凿
pliers	*qiánzi*	钳子
hammer	*chuí*	锤
saw	*jùchuáng*	锯床
tape measure	*juǎnchǐ*	卷尺
small lock	*xiǎosuǒ*	小锁

Although cheap and high-quality tailoring is widely available in China, a knowledge of modern Western style is not, and it is unlikely that you will want to have any important wardrobe item made except at the tailor shop in a tourist hotel, where the negotiations will take place in English. The following items might be needed to supplement your wardrobe while traveling, and can be purchased at department stores.

I'd like to buy a **long-sleeved shirt**.
*Wǒ xiángmǎi yíjiàn **chángxiù chènshān**.*
我想买一件长袖衬衫.

short-sleeved shirt	*duǎnxiù chènshān*	短袖衬衫
overcoat	*dàyī*	大衣
raincoat	*yǔyī*	雨衣
anorak	*dài fēngmàode hòu jiākè*	带风帽的 厚夹克
briefs	*sānjiǎokù*	三角裤
undershirts	*nèiyī*	内衣
trousers	*kùzi*	裤子
jeans	*niúzǎikù*	牛仔裤
shorts	*duǎnkù*	短裤
sweater	*máoxiànshān*	毛线衫
sweatshirt	*tàotóushān*	套头衫
padded jacket	*miánǎo*	棉袄
swimming trunks	*yóuyǒngkù*	游泳裤
sports jacket	*yùndòngshān*	运动衫
suit	*yīfú (tàozhuāng)*	衣服(套装)

If you can settle on a suitable fabric, your Chinese tailor or dressmaker will easily be able to replicate an item brought from home as a model; otherwise, the same advice listed under "Men's Clothing" applies. Remember that Chinese sizes are metric, and can be a bit erratic. See pp. 146–47 for other expressions useful when purchasing clothing.

I'd like to buy a **dress**.
*Wǒ xiángmǎi yíjiàn **liányīqún**.*
我想买一件连衣裙.

blouse	*nǔchènshān*	女衬衫
skirt	*qúnzi*	裙子
panties	*nèikù*	内裤
bra	*xiōngzhào*	胸罩
jeans	*niúzǎikù*	牛仔裤
shorts	*duǎnkù*	短裤
sweater	*máoxiànshān*	毛线衫
sweatshirt	*tàotóushān*	套头衫
padded jacket	*miánǎo*	棉袄
bathing cap	*yóuyǒngmào*	游泳帽
swimming suit	*yóuyǒngyī*	游泳衣
overcoat	*dàyī*	大衣
raincoat	*yǔyī*	雨衣

China travel is rough on shoes and you may wish to pick up a extra pair on an extended trip. Although what is offered may not appear on the cutting edge of fashion, remember that this is where most of our sport shoes are made. Chinese are fairly informal dressers; sportcoats for men and skirts for women are adequate for even the poshest affairs. The necktie listed below would likely be for a souvenir.

I'd like to buy some **leather shoes**.
*Wǒ xiángmǎi **píxié**.*
我想买皮鞋.

hiking boots	*lǚyóuxié*	旅遊鞋
tennis shoes	*qiúxié*	球鞋
socks	*wàzi*	袜子
stockings	*chángtǒngwà*	长统袜
panty hose	*chángwà (duǎnwà)*	长袜(短袜)
gloves	*shǒutào*	手套
handkerchief	*shǒupà*	手帕
scarf	*wéijīn*	围巾
necktie	*lǐngdài*	领带
wallet	*qiánbāo*	钱包
handbag	*shǒutíbāo*	手提包
briefcase	*shǒutíxiāng*	手提箱
suitcase	*yīxiāng*	衣箱
umbrella	*yúsǎn*	雨伞

Although modern Chinese costume jewelry may have little appeal, interesting items are offered at antique shops and and street markets. Jade varies widely in quality and value; it is unwise to make an expensive acquisition without expert help.

I want to buy a **ring**.
Wǒ xiángmǎi ge jièzhi.
我想买个戒指.

bracelet	*shǒuzhuó*	手镯
brooch	*xiōngzhēn*	胸针
necklace	*xiàngliàn*	项链
earrings	*ěrhuán*	耳环
pendant	*chuíshì*	垂饰

Do you have something in **jade**?
Nín yǒu yù zhìpǐn ma?
您有玉制品吗?

emerald	*lǜbǎoshí*	绿宝石
aquamarine	*shuǐlánbǎoshí*	水兰宝石
amethyst	*zǐjīng*	紫晶
diamond	*zuànshí*	钻石
pearl	*zhēnzhū*	珍珠
ruby	*hóngbǎoshí*	红宝石
sapphire	*lánbǎoshí*	兰宝石
turquoise	*lǜsōngshí*	绿松石
gold	*jīn*	金
silver	*yín*	银

What is that stone?
Nà shì shénme bǎoshi?
那是什么宝石?

Familiar brands will likely be displayed only at hotel shops and Friendship Stores. If you are in an experimental or budget-conscious mood, however, you may wish to seek out the Chinese equivalents of your favorite preparations.

I want to buy an **eyebrow pencil.**
*Wǒ xiángmǎi yìzhī **miáo yǎnméide qiānbǐ**.*
我想买一支描眼眉的铅笔.

nail polish	*zhíjiā yóu*	指甲油
nail polish remover	*qù zhíjiā yóují*	去指甲油剂
emery boards	*bǎoshā bǎn*	宝砂板
lipstick	*kǒuhóng*	口红
moistening cream	*rùnfū shuāng*	润肤霜
mascara	*jiémáoyóu*	睫毛油
foundation	*dǐsè*	底色
cologne	*xiāngshuǐ*	香水
blusher	*yānzhǐ*	胭脂
eye shadow	*miáo yǎnbǐ*	描眼笔
hairbrush	*shuāzi*	刷子
comb	*shūzi*	梳子
mirror	*jìngzi*	镜子
hand cream	*cāshǒu yóu*	擦手油
tissues	*miánzhǐ*	棉纸

Chinese cosmetics and toiletries are typically displayed on the ground floor of most department stores, while first-aid supplies and non-prescription medicines are found in pharmacies. For these latter, see pp. 184–85.

I want to buy some **deodorant.**
*Wǒ xiǎngmǎi **qúxiùjì**.*
我想买驱臭剂.

cologne	*xiāngshuǐ*	香水
condoms	*bìyùntào*	闭孕套
toothbrush	*yáshuā*	牙刷
toothpaste	*yágāo*	牙膏
razor	*guāhú dāo*	刮胡刀
razor blade	*dāopiàn*	刀片
nail clippers	*zhǐjiǎ dāo*	指甲刀
insect repellent	*qùwénjì*	驱蚊剂
lip balm	*chúngāo*	唇膏
mouthwash	*shùkǒujì*	漱口剂
toilet paper	*shóuzhǐ*	手纸
sanitary napkins	*wèishēngzhǐ*	卫生纸
tampons	*wèishēng miángùn*	卫生棉棍
scissors	*jiǎndāo*	剪刀
shampoo	*xǐfàjì*	洗发剂
soap	*féizào*	肥皂
soap dish	*féizàohé*	肥皂盒

Money Matters

With the abolishment of the cumbersome FECs (Foreign Exchange Certificates, a scrip created especially for use by tourists), handling money in the People's Republic has become greatly simplified. Still, simple daily transactions can pose difficulties as simple as having or getting the right change. The smaller denominations of *rénmínbǐ*, literally "the people's money," can be hard to come by, especially when exchanging currency at authorized venues—banks and tourist hotels. You will usually be given the largest bills possible to make up the required sum; try to get some *língqián*, "small change" on the spot. Street vendors and even established stores are often unable to give change for large notes.

Rénmínbǐ paper money is issued in notes of one, two, five, ten, fifty, and one-hundred *yuán,* as well as one, two, and five *jiǎo,* and one, two, and five *fēn.* The bills decrease in size, but increase in decrepitude, with decreasing value, and can create quite an unruly pile. Take your time when paying and counting change; the average Chinese street vendor is not burdened by the moral dilemma of short-changing unwary foreigners. There are coins as well for one *yuán,* five *jiǎo,* and one, two, and five *fēn.* The *fēn* coins and bills can be stashed in a separate pocket; they are useful only for bus fares and the most modest sundries.

When away from main cities, you cannot count on being able to exchange money at any time. Verify that at times posted for currency exchange at your hotel someone will be on duty; if you see someone at the currency-exchange counter, take advantage of the opportunity. Always carry enough (or have stashed away enough) to tide you over for a few days. Traveler's checks are widely recognized and fine for carrying larger amounts safely, but it is good to have a modest amount of dollars, in small bills, set aside for emergencies. They are also quite useful for bargaining in free markets in outlying areas—Tibet, for example—where they are the currency of choice.

When bargaining—and you should always bargain outside of department stores, luxury hotel shops, and restaurants with fixed prices—ask that the price be written down. Carry a pencil and small pad of paper for this purpose and counter with your own written offer. At government-owned outlets such as the craft "factories," most guidebooks advise that no bargaining is allowed. However, this is no longer true; the decentralization of decision-making authority that has characterized the Chinese economy in general recently is working in your favor. Local operations, pressed to turn a profit on their own, will often cut a bargain to do so, especially on more expensive items. If you are with a group, you may have to be discreet, or return without your companions to close the deal. As always with bargaining, be persistent, polite, and prepared to walk away.

Getting It Done

This chapter deals with the routine services you may need while traveling in China, as well as those you may require in an emergency (for emergencies, see p. 186–87 and "Fingertips" in this chapter).

At the outset, let's be honest and say that while China may be a fascinating country, it is not an easy place to get things done. This is partly because, as previously mentioned, a Communist economy does not provide much incentive for service workers to go out of their way for anyone. But it is also because the Chinese just don't do things the way we do. What ever you want done will likely take a bit longer, be a bit more complicated, and probably require some paperwork.

Your best bet for avoiding hassles is preparation. Bring with you to China a generous supply of any special consumables you may require—food, drink, medicine, film, batteries, etc. All your equipment, whether camera, watch, electric razor, or hair dryer, should be in good repair and you should have the proper adapters for 220 volts, 60 cycles, and plugs. (Several types of outlet are used in China, so an "international" kit with a variety of adapters is recommended.)

If you do have need of a particular service, the deluxe tourist hotel is your best friend, filled as it is with English-speaking Chinese who are used to the strange requests of foreigners. The bigger the establishment the better: four-star Western-style complexes in Beijing, Xian, and Shanghai will have beauty parlors and barber shops, bookstores and newsstands, English-speaking medical professionals, and full concierge services. Outside main cities, however, these will not be easily found, so plan accordingly. The expressions listed in this chapter should get most common needs attended to. The following should at least help get you started toward right place:

Could you tell me where the closest **bank** is?
*Fùjìn shénme dìfāng yǒu **yínháng**?*
附近什么地方有银行？

barber	*lǐfàshī*	理发师
beauty parlor	*měiróngtīng*	美容厅
CITS office	*Zhōngguó Guójì Lǚxíngshè*	中国国际 社旅行
currency exchange	*wàichāo duìhuàn*	外钞兑换
doctor	*yīshēng*	医生
dentist	*yáyī*	牙医
hospital	*yīyuàn*	医院
laundry	*xǐyīdiàn*	洗衣店
pharmacy	*yàofáng*	药房
police station	*jǐngchájú*	警察局
post office	*yóujú*	邮局
shoe repair	*xiūxié diàn*	修鞋店
tailor	*cáiféng diàn*	裁缝店
travel service	*lǚyóujú*	旅遊局

The Chinese can fix anything, although the quality of repairs can range from excellent to crudely practical: that hole in your luggage can be fixed, but you might not like the way your bag looks afterward. For tailoring or repair of cameras, watches, jewelry, or other valuables, it's better to wait until you get back home, if possible.

Tipping is theoretically prohibited in China, and in fact is not the custom in restaurants or for taxis. However, Chinese do have a tradition of consideration for services rendered, and it is useful to offer some gratuity—up front rather than later—in those instances where the service you require may be difficult (tickets to a popular performance) or vital (delivering your luggage to you at the airport). Use common sense and be discreet so as not to embarrass the recipient in front of others. At the same time, gratuities for CITS guides have gotten totally out of hand, with, sometimes, demands for a certain amount per day per guide (often accompanied by a hard luck story about how their bosses will expect and confiscate the greater portion). My inclination is to tip good guides well and stiff the bad ones. Whether this will result in any lessons learned is debatable, but it satisfies a need for some personal guidelines. Most visitors to China are on vacation and should be relieved of the burden of feeling either guilty or ripped off.

The national travel services of China were originally state monopolies set up to cater to different types of tourists: China International Travel Services (CITS) for non-Chinese (and non-Chinese-speaking) groups; China Travel Service (CTS) for overseas Chinese visitors; and China Youth Travel Service (CYTS) for student groups. With economic decentralization, however, these organizations have come into competition, and you can request help for tickets and accommodations from any of them, regardless of your age and nationality and even if you are not traveling on a group tour arranged by them.

Of course, you will be charged for their services, and there will be a surcharge on the tickets they purchase because you are a foreigner. Moreover, such services have always been erratic, sometimes obsequiously helpful, other times a complete ripoff. It is really impossible to evaluate how worthwhile it will be to deal with these organizations; you simply have to ask around among your fellow travelers and decide, for example, how many extra dollars given to CITS is worth how many extra hours standing in line at the train station.

I should point out that I have had much better luck with local organizations, especially those for Tibetan tourism in Lhasa and Xinjiang tourism in Urumqi. They were mostly staffed by locals rather than Han Chinese and seemed to evince a greater interest in ensuring that visitors have a successful trip in their areas. For expressions useful for making travel arrangements, see Chapter 3.

If your standards are strict, head for a beauty parlor at a big tourist hotel. See "Barber Shop" on the next page for other useful expressions.

Where can I get my hair done?
Qǐngwèn nár yǒu fàláng?
请问哪儿有发廊？

Where is a beauty parlor?
Měiróngtīng zài nǎr?
美容厅在哪儿？

Can you make an appointment for me?
Qǐng géi wǒ dìng ge yùyuē hǎo ma?
请给我定个预约好吗？

I'd like a **shampoo and set**.
Wó xiǎng bǎ tóufa xǐ chuī dìngxíng.
我想把头发洗吹定型．

permanent	*tàngfà*	烫发
body wave	*dìngxíng*	定型
haircut	*jiǎnfà*	剪发
manicure	*rǎnzhíjia*	染指甲
pedicure	*xiūjiǎo*	修脚

I want it to look like this.
Wó xiǎngyào zhèige yàngzi.
我想要这个样子．

How long is the wait?
Yào děng duōjiǔ?
要等多久．

How long will it take?
Yào yòng duōjiǔ?
要用多久．

Again, if your standards are strict, head for a barber at a main tourist hotel. Or, for a real adventure in grooming, try getting a haircut and shave at an outdoor barber.

Where can I get my haircut?
Wǒ zài nǎr kéyǐ lǐfà?
我在哪可以理发？

Is there a barber shop nearby?
Fùjìn yóu lǐfàguǎn ma?
附近有理发馆吗？

I'd like a **haircut**.
Wó xiǎng lǐge fà.
我想理个发.

shave	*guāliǎn*	刮脸
trim	*jiǎnfà*	剪发
shampoo	*xǐfàjì*	洗发剂
manicure	*xiū zhíjiǎ*	修指甲

I part my hair here.
Wǒ zài zhàr fēnyìn.
我在这儿分印.

Take a little more off here.
Zhàr zài duō jiǎn diǎn.
这儿再多剪点.

It looks fine.
Búcuò.
不错.

Laundry services are available at the service desk at most hotels. Your room should have a laundry bag and forms for cleaning instructions. Services vary widely in quality and price, with the better hotels charging as much as in Europe.

Is there a laundry service?
Yǒu xǐyīdiàn ma?
有洗衣店吗?

I want these washed and folded.
Qǐng bǎ zhèxiē yīfu xíhǎo diéhǎo.
请把这些衣服洗好叠好.

I want these ironed.
Qǐng bǎ zhèxiē yīfu yùnyíxià.
请把这些衣服熨一下.

I want these dry cleaned.
Qǐng gānxǐ.
请干洗.

I want this mended.
Qǐng bǔyíxià.
请补一下.

I want this stain removed.
Qǐng bǎ wūdiǎn qùdiào.
请把污点去掉.

Most important is alerting the service desk attendant that you have laundry (drop it off yourself rather than leave it in the room to be picked up), and determining what time it will be ready. It is best to get it done at least a day before a fixed departure.

Is there a laundry nearby?
Fùjìn yóu xǐyīdiàn ma?
附近有先衣店吗？

Is there a dry cleaner nearby?
Fùjìn yǒu gānxǐdiàn ma?
附近有干洗店吗？

When will they be ready?
Shénme shíjiān kěyí qǔ?
什么时间可以取？

I need them right away.
Wǒ mǎshàng xūyào zhèxiē yīfu.
我马上需要这些衣服.

I must have them back tonight.
Wǒ bìxū jīnwǎn qǔ.
我必须今晚取.

I'm leaving tomorrow.
Wǒ míngtiān zǒu.
我明天走.

Chinese tailoring, like Chinese repairs, can be excellent or crudely practical. If you must have high quality, it would be better to take the garment home with you rather than take a chance.

Is there a tailor around here?
Fùjìn yǒu cáiféng ma?
附近有裁缝吗？

Can you recommend a good tailor?
Gěi wǒ jièshào ge hǎo cáiféng, hǎoma?
给我介绍个好裁缝，好吗？

Can you fix this?
Nǐ néng bǎ zhège bǔyíxià ma?
你能把这个补一下吗？

I'd like to have these **shortened**.
*Qíng bǎ zhèxiē **shōuduándiǎn**.*
请把这些收短点？

lengthened	*fàngchángdiǎn*	放长点
altered	*gǎiyíxià*	改一下
mended	*bǔyíxià*	补一下

When will it be ready?
Shénme shíjiān kéyí qǔ?
什么时间可以取？

When should I come back?
Wǒ shénme shíjiān láiná?
我什么时间来拿？

Most shoe repairs in China are handled by outdoor vendors who gather at busy places such as markets. Again, repairs may be crude but will be effective.

Where can I get my shoes polished?
Wǒ zài nǎr kéyǐ cāxié?
我在哪儿可以擦鞋?

Where can I get my shoes repaired?
Wǒ zài nǎr kéyǐ xīuxié?
我在哪儿可以修鞋?

Is there a shoe repair place nearby?
Fùjìn yǒu xīuxiédiàn ma?
附近有修鞋店吗?

Where can I get this fixed?
Zài nǎr kéyǐ bǎ zhège xiūyíxià?
在哪儿可以把这个修一下?

I want new **soles**.
*Wǒ xiǎng huàn **xiédǐ**.*
我想换鞋底.

| heels | *xiégēn* | 鞋跟 |
| soles and heels | *xiédǐ hé xiégēn* | 鞋底和鞋跟 |

Can you do it while I wait?
Wǒ děngzhe nǐ xiūhǎo, xíngma?
我等着你修好, 行吗.

How much will it cost?
Duōshǎo qián?
多少钱?

The Chinese postal service is excellent, typically delivering within China in one or two days. International airmail should reach its destination in about a week. International rates for letters and small packets (up to two kilos) are the same to all countries, and there is a lower rate for printed matter.

I'd like to buy stamps for international letters.
Wǒ xiángmǎi hángkōng yóupiào.
我想买航空邮票.

I'd like stamps for international postcards.
Wǒ xiángmǎi hángkōng míngxìnpiàn yóupiào.
我想买航空明信片邮票.

I'd like to buy some air letters.
Wǒ xiángmǎi hángkōng xìnjiān.
我想买航空信笺.

I want to send this **letter**.
Wǒ xiáng bǎ zhè fēngxìn jìzǒu.
我想把这封信寄走.

postcard	*míngxìnpiàn*	明信片
small packet	*xiǎo yóubāo*	小邮包
parcel	*bāoguǒ*	包裹
printed matter	*yìnshuāpǐn*	印刷品

I want to send this **air mail**.
Wǒ xiáng bǎ zhègè jì hángkōng.
我想把这个寄航空.

sea mail	*hǎiyùn*	海运
registered mail	*guàhào xìn*	挂号信
parcel post	*bāoguǒ yóujì*	包裹邮寄

If speed is all important, there is an EMS (International Express Mail) service offered, with rates varying from country to country. In addition, the major private express mail companies (UPS, DHL, FedEx, etc.) are operating in major cities.

I want to send this by International Express Mail.
Wó xiăngyòng Guójì Jiākuài Yóujì zhège.
我想用国际加快邮寄这个.

I want to send this the cheapest way.
Wó xiăngyòng zuì piányide fāngfă jì zhège.
我想用最便宜的方法寄这个.

Inside are **books**.
*Lǐmiàn shì **shū**.*
里面是书.

gifts	*lǐpǐn*	礼品
clothes	*yīfu*	衣服

There is nothing of value inside.
Lǐmiàn méi shénme zhíqiánde dōngxi.
里面没什么值钱的东西.

I'd like to insure this.
Wŏ xiánggěi zhèige báoxiăn.
我想给这个保险.

How much is the postage?
Yóufèi duōshăo?
邮费多少?

How long will it take to get there?
Zhèi yào duōcháng shíjiān néng dào?
这要多长时间能到?

Although Chinese are avid photographers, Chinese film and processing are of uneven quality. Modern processing facilities for Fuji and Kodak color prints are available, but slides should be taken home for developing.

Where can I get film developed?
Nǎr yǒu chōngxǐ jiāojuǎnde dìfāng?
哪有冲洗胶卷的地方？

I'd like to get these developed.
Wǒ xiǎng bǎ zhèxiē juǎn chōngle.
我想把这些卷冲了．

I'd like glossy prints.
Wǒ yào biǎomiàn guānghuáde.
我要表面光滑的．

I'd like matte-finished prints.
Wǒ yào biǎomiàn wú guāngzéde.
我要表面无光泽的．

How much is it per roll?
Yìjuǎn duóshǎo qián?
一卷多少钱？

When can I pick them up?
Shénme shíjiān qǔ?
什么时间取？

I'd like a copy of this one.
Wǒ xiǎng bǎ zhège zài yìn yìzhāng.
我想把这个再印一张．

Two prints each, please.   (Numbers, p. 22)
Qǐng yìn yíshì liǎngfèn.
请印一式两分．

Yes, the Chinese are capable of repairing or jury-rigging almost anything (watch the street mechanics fix bicycles!), but again, finding the person who can handle your problem will take time and luck.

This doesn't work.
Zhège huàile.
这个坏了.

I'd like to get this fixed.
Qíng bǎ zhège xiūlǐ yíxià.
请把这个修理一下?

Can this be fixed?
Zhège hái néng xiūhǎo ma?
这个还能修好吗?

How much will it cost?
Yào huā duōshǎo qián?
要花多少钱?

How much will a new one cost?
Xīnde yào huā duōshǎo qián?
新的要花多少钱?

How long will it take?
Xūyào duōshǎo shíjiān?
需要多少时间?

Can you do it while I wait?
Wǒ zài zhèr děngzhe nín xiū, hǎoma?
我在这儿等着您修, 好吗?

The business centers set up in most tourist hotels are your best bet for these services. If you are not a guest of the hotel, you need not mention this.

Where is the business center?
Fúwù zhōngxīn zài nǎr?
服务中心在哪儿?

Where can I send a fax?
Wǒ zài nǎr kéyǐ sòng chuánzhēn?
我在哪儿可以送传真?

Where can I get some copies made?
Wǒ zài nǎr kéyǐ fùyìn?
我在哪儿可以复印?

Where can I make an international call?
Wǒ zài nǎr kéyǐ dǎ guójì chángtú?
我在哪儿可以打国际长途?

I'd like to send a fax.
Wǒ xiángdǎ ge chuánzhēn.
我想打个传真.

Here's the number.
Zhèshì diànhuà hàomǎ.
这是电话号码.

What's the country code for [COUNTRY]?
[COUNTRY] *guójiā de hàomǎ shì shénme?*
[COUNTRY]国家的号码是什么?

f the fax or copier of the business center is out of
rder, try the business office of the hotel, which
ften has the same equipment.

'd like to call this number.
Wǒ xiǎngdǎ zhège hàomǎ.
我想打这个号码.

'd like to call collect.
Qǐng géi wǒ jiē duìfāng fùkuǎn diànhuà.
请给我接对方负款电话.

'd like to get some copies made.
Wǒ xiǎng fùyìn xiē dōngxi.
我想复印些东西.

need **one** copy of each.   (Numbers, p. 22)
*Qǐng yíshì **yífèn**.*
请一式一分.

'd like to make it smaller.
Wǒ xiáng bǎ zhège suō xiǎo xiē.
我想把这个缩小些.

'd like to make it larger.
Wǒ xiáng bǎ zhège fàngdà xiē.
我想把这个放大些.

low much is it per copy?
Měi zhāng duōshǎo qián?
每张多少钱?

lease charge my room.
Qǐng gēn wǒde fángjiān suàn zài yìqǐ.
请跟我的房间算在一起.

In an emergency, go straight to a main hospital or a large hotel with a clinic. If you are with a tour group, insist that your CITS guide arrange for someone to translate for you.

I must see a doctor.
Wǒ děikàn yīshēng.
我得看医生.

Is there a doctor who speaks English?
Yǒu méi yǒu huì jiǎng Yīngwénde yīshēng?
有没有会讲英文的医生?

Does anyone speak English?
Yǒu huì jiǎng Yīngwénde méi yǒu?
有会讲英文的有没?

It hurts here. / It hurts when I do this.
Zhèr téng. / Wǒ zhè yàng de shíhòu téng.
这儿疼. / 我这样的时候疼.

I feel nauseous. / I've been vomiting.
Wǒ xiǎng tù. / Wǒ yìzhí zài tù.
我想吐. / 我一直在吐.

I'm having a heart attack.
Wǒ xīnzàng fàn bìngle.
我心脏犯病了.

Do you know what's wrong?
Nín shuō bìngyīn shì shéme?
您说病因是什么?

Is it serious?
Yánzhòng ma?
严重么?

Medical services in China are extremely inexpensive by Western standards. As a foreigner, you will pay a surcharge at a hospital, but you will get faster service.

I hurt myself.
Wǒ shāngle wǒ zìjǐ.
我伤了我自己.

cut myself	*lále wǒ zìjǐ*	拉了我自己
burned myself	*shāole wǒ zìjǐ*	烧了我自己
fell down	*shuāi dǎole*	率倒了

I have a fever.
Wǒ zài fāshāo.
我在发烧.

cold	*lěng*	冷
chills	*fālěng*	发冷
the flu	*gǎnmào*	感冒
a headache	*tóuténg*	头疼
a stomachache	*wèiténg*	胃疼
indigestion	*xiāohuà bùhǎo*	消化不好
constipation	*dàbiàn gānzào*	大便干燥
diarrhea	*xièdù*	泻肚
chest pains	*xiōngténg*	胸疼
a sore throat	*sǎngzi téng*	嗓子疼
an eye irritation	*yǎnjīng shànghuǒ*	眼睛上火
some dizziness	*yǒu diǎn tóuyūn*	有点头晕
ringing ears	*ěrmíng*	耳鸣

Can I continue on the tour?
Wǒ néng jìxù lǚyóu ma?
我能继续旅遊吗?

As with doctors, it is best to find an English-speaking dentist through a recommendation from the hotel desk.

I need a dentist who speaks English.
Wǒ xūyào yíge huìshuō Yīngwénde yáyī.
我需要一个会说英文的牙医.

Would you make an appointment for me?
Qǐng géi wǒ dìngge yùyuē, hǎoma?
请给我定个预约, 好吗?

Please write down the name and address.
Qǐng bǎ xìngmíng, dìzhǐ xiěyíxià.
请把姓名, 地址写一下.

I have a toothache.
Wǒ yáténg.
我牙疼.

It hurts right here.
Zhàr téng.
这儿疼.

I broke a tooth.
Wǒ gèsuìle yìkē yá.
我硌碎了一颗牙.

I've lost a filling.
Wó bǔde nàkē yá huàile.
我补的那颗牙坏了.

Can you fix this?
Nín néng búhǎo zhège ma?
您能补好这个吗?

Traditional Chinese medicine is based on five millennia of practice, and you may wish to test its effectiveness. You may either see a doctor of Chinese medicine, or ask the pharmacist at a Chinese herbal medicine shop to prescribe a remedy.

I would like to see a doctor of Chinese medicine.
Wó xiǎngkàn Zhōngyī.
我想看中医.

Where is a Chinese pharmacy?
Zhōngyàofáng zài nǎr?
中药房在哪儿?

I have a **headache**. (Doctors, p. 181)
Wǒ zài tóuténg.
我在头疼.

Can you give me something for a **headache**?
Nín néng géi wǒ diǎn zhì tóuténg de yào ma?
您能给我点治头疼的药吗?

Where can I get acupuncture?
Nár yǒu zhēn jiǔ zhìliáo?
哪有针灸治疗?

Where can I get a massage?
Nár yǒu ànmó?
哪有按摩?

Can I make an appointment?
Wǒ kéyǐ dìngge yùyuē ma?
我可以定个预约吗?

How much is it?
Duōshǎo qián?
多少钱?

Chinese drugstores typically sell only products relating directly to health and hygiene, with toiletries and beauty products found more readily in department stores (see p. 160).

Where is a pharmacy?
Yàofáng zài nǎr?
药房在哪儿?

I need some **aspirin**.
Wǒ xūyào āsīpǐlín.
我需要阿司匹林.

adhesive tape	*jiāobù*	胶布
antibiotics	*kàngjūnsù*	抗菌素
antiseptic	*xiāodújì*	消毒剂
band aids	*chuàngkětiē*	创可贴
cotton swaps	*miánqiú*	棉球
condoms	*bìyùntào*	避孕套
cough drops	*zhǐké sù*	止咳素
cough medicine	*zhǐké jì*	止咳剂
ear drops	*ěrduō yào*	耳朵药
eye drops	*yǎnyàoshuǐ*	眼药水
gauze	*shābù*	纱布
insect repellent	*qūwén jì*	驱蚊剂
laxative	*tōngbiàn jì*	通便剂
mouthwash	*shùkǒu jì*	漱口剂
razor blades	*tìxūdāo*	剃须刀
sanitary napkins	*wèishēng jīn*	卫生巾
tampons	*wèishēng miángùn*	卫生棉棍
thermometer	*wēndù jì*	温度计
throat lozenges	*hándiǎn*	含碘
toothpaste	*yágāo*	牙膏

You will find both Western and Oriental pharmacies (shops selling herbal preparations) in China, in some cases simply opposite counters in the same store.

I need something for a **cold**.
Wǒ xūyào diǎn gǎnmào yào.
我需要点感冒药.

cough	*késù*	咳嗽
constipation	*biànmì*	便秘
diarrhea	*xièdù*	泻肚
earache	*ěrténg*	耳疼
fever	*fāshāo*	发烧
hay fever	*huāfěnrè*	花粉热
headache	*tóuténg*	头疼
stomachache	*wèiténg*	胃疼
indigestion	*xiāohuà bù liáng*	消化不良
insect bites	*wéndīng*	蚊叮
motion sickness	*tóuyūn*	头晕
runny nose	*liúbítì*	流鼻涕
sore throat	*sǎngzi téng*	嗓子疼
sunburn	*rìzhuó*	日炙

When should I take these?
Shénme shíjiān chī?
什么时间吃?

How many should I take each time?
Wǒ měicì chī jǐpiàn?
我每次吃几片?

How often should I take these?
Měi gé duócháng shíjiān chī yícì?
每隔多长时间吃一次?

You can dial 110 for police emergencies in all major cities, but expect assistance in Chinese only. For additional information useful in emergencies, see "Fingertips," p. 188.

Please help me!
Jiù mìng!
救命！

This is an emergency!
Jǐnjí qíngkuàng!
紧急情况！

Please call the **police**!
*Qǐng jiào **jǐngchá**!*
请叫警察！

a doctor	*yīshēng*	医生
fire department	*xiāofáng zhàn*	消防站

Please take me to the police.
Qǐng dài wǒ dào jǐngchájú.
请带我到警察局.

a doctor	*yīshēng*	医生
a hospital	*yīyuàn*	医院

Where is the nearest hospital?
Zuìjìnde yīyuàn zài nǎr?
最近的医院在哪儿？

Where is the nearest Public Security Bureau?
Zuìjìnde Gōngānjú zài nǎr?
最近的公安局在哪儿？

You can dial 119 for fire emergencies in all major cities, but expect assistance in Chinese only. If you report a crime, allow plenty of time for the inevitable paperwork.

I want to report a **fire**.
Zháo huǒle.
着火了.

an accident	*chūshile*	出事了
a robbery	*qiǎngjié*	抢劫
a fight	*dǎjià*	打骂

Someone **is having a heart attack**.
Yǒu rén fàn xīnzàng bìngle.
有人犯心脏病了.

choking	*yē zháole*	噎着了
can't breathe	*zhìxī*	窒息
is bleeding severely	*dà chūxuě*	大出血
has had an accident	*chūshile*	出事了

Stop, thief!
Zhuā xiǎotōu ya!
抓小偷呀!

I've been robbed.
Wǒ bèi tōule!
我被偷了!

Someone stole my **wallet**.
Yǒu rén tōule wǒde qiánbāo.
有人偷了我的钱包.

money	*qián*	钱
traveler's checks	*lǚyóu zhīpiào*	旅遊支票
passport	*hùzhào*	护照
suitcase	*shǒutíxiāng*	手提箱

Health and Medical

The first rule, of course, is don't drink the water. This stricture actually doesn't present much of a problem in China, as even the natives don't drink it. Water is boiled and delivered in carafes to your hotel room every morning, and bottled spring water is available all over. In spite of the best precautions, however, visitors to China often come down with something or other over the course of several weeks of travel, usually intestinal (simple diarrhea, mostly due to lots of oily food) or respiratory (again not serious, mostly due to strange new bugs the lungs are exposed to, aggravated by dust in the air).

However, there are more serious health hazards, especially for those traveling in remote areas. These include hepatitis and epidemics of cholera, and in Tibet, altitude sickness and giardia, a severe diarrhea caused by amoeba. Travelers to those areas should certainly consult their doctors beforehand. And, of course, any symptoms persistent or recurring should be looked into. Here, your best bet is a clinic at a main tourist hotel or an English-speaking doctor recommended by the hotel.

The medical phrases listed in *Fingertip Chinese* are intended only as a backup if you cannot get a consultation in English. Do not rely on them in case of a serious illness. If you are in a group, demand that CITS provide you with an interpreter; if you are traveling on your own, request an interpreter, whom you will pay for.

Passports and Valuables

Although China is a safe country for travel, it is becoming less so as the nation moves toward more individual economic freedom and the disparity between rich and poor increases. Still, tourists are rarely the victim of violent crimes; they are more often the prey of pickpockets, purse slashers, and petty thieves. Against these types, common sense is your best weapon. Don't take unnecessary valuables with you to China. Expensive watches and jewelry are simply not needed. Wear a money belt or vest with a zippered inside pocket for passports and valuables. Watch out especially in the crowds that gather for buying tickets and boarding transportation. Keep checked baggage locked when in transit, as required, and do not ship money and valuables in them. Hotel rooms are generally safe, but again, you may wish to lock your bags when you are out of your room for the day. Hotels will also have safe-deposit boxes available.

The police of China are a national organization called the Public Security Bureau (PSB), or *Gōng-ānjú*. They can be reached in emergencies by dialing 110 in most cities, but cannot be counted on to understand your English; get a Chinese to call. When you report a crime, count on spending some time to make out the complaint; usually an official of the foreign affairs section of the PSB must first be summoned. Ask for a copy of the report if you need it for an insurance claim back home, or to replace stolen traveler's checks.

For Further Information

Group Travel

Deluxe, escorted package tours to China are offered by a number of reputable travel agents. Since a tour of China can cost anywhere from $2500 to $7000, more than the usual care should be taken when booking. To see China in a three-week tour is in fact a rather presumptuous undertaking; imagine booking a three-week "tour" of North America. Obviously only a few highlights can be seen in a short trip, so make sure that those places you are particularly interested in visiting are included. On the other hand, when reviewing itineraries, remember that in China each transfer to a new city typically requires a full travel day; thus more places does not necessarily make a better tour. Less than three days per stop (five to seven destinations in a three-week tour) will create a pace that most would consider too rushed.

Your group will be assigned Chinese "national guide" for the duration of the tour, as well as a "local guide" in each city. Unfortunately, the quality of guides in general has gone downhill from the early days (c. 1980s) of China tourism, when "foreign guests" (and their hard currency) were so assiduously courted. In all fairness, many guides are pleasant and helpful; however, they cannot be counted on to have the knowledge and communicative skills most visitors will expect. To avoid disappointment, book a tour led by an authority on China who will lecture the group. Inquire about the leader's academic specialty (art, religion, modern China, etc.) for the tour will probably be shaped to his or her interests. If the tour is not accompanied by a lecturer (or even if it is), bring some relevant reading material (see "A Traveler's Library for China" on p. 194).

Finally, of course, the usual precautions when dealing with travel agents apply: before making a deposit, check the company's record with the Better Business Bureau, and invest in trip insurance.

Individual Travel

You will certainly get a different and perhaps truer impression of modern China if you go on your own, without a group. However, be prepared to spend lots more time hassling with travel arrangements and accommodations. To obtain a Chinese visa, a passport valid for six months, with blank pages, and a passport-size photo are required. Fees in the U.S. for American citizens range from $30 for a single-entry visa to $80 for a multiple-entry visa good for one year. Normal waiting time is from three days to one week, although faster service, according to a schedule of surcharges, is available. Contact numbers:

Chicago (312) 573 3070
Hong Kong 585 1794
Houston (713) 524 0778
London (071) 636 2580
Melbourne (03) 822 0604
New York (212) 330 7409

San Francisco (415) 563 4885
Washington (202) 328 2500

The China Travel Service (CTS) was originally set up to help overseas Chinese with their China travel plans, while the China International Travel Service (CITS, and called the China National Tourist Office outside of China) catered to other foreign guests. Now, however, they are in competition and either may be contacted for assistance with travel arrangements. Contact numbers:

CITS
Hong Kong 732 5888
London (071) 935 9427
Los Angeles (818) 545 7505
New York (212) 867 0271
Sydney (02) 299 4057

CTS
Hong Kong 521 7163
Jakarta (21) 629 4256
Kuala Lumpur (03) 242 7077
Los Angeles (818) 288 8222
San Francisco (415) 398 6627
Singapore 224 0550
Sydney (02) 211 2633
Vancouver (604) 872-8787

Partially Booked Trips

It is possible now for the individual traveler with a modest budget to book a personalized but limited itinerary in advance, without shelling out the exorbitant sums demanded by CITS. All the main cities of China are now served by air directly from Hong Kong; visas can be obtained and inexpensive accommodations in tourist hotels in most cities booked from there as well. Thus one could arrange a two- or three-city tour (say Xian, Beijing, and Shanghai), staying three or four days in each place and returning to Hong Kong. In these larger cities, one can take advantage of the day excursions offered by the hotel tour desks to nearby sites (to the Qin Pits in Xian, to the Great Wall and Ming Tombs in Beijing, to gardens of Suzhou from Shanghai). You can furthermore arrange your flights entering and leaving China on Dragonair, owned jointly by the PRC and Hong Kong-based Cathay Pacific, and thus avoid the generally poorer service of CAAC (which costs no less).

When making arrangements by this method, however, you will not be able to book the cheapest accommodations available, such as dorm rooms; nor can you book China's best travel bargains, such as hard sleepers for overnight train travel. Still, such a "partially booked" itinerary can afford an excellent compromise between the regimentation of group touring and the hassles of low-budget solo travel. Useful Hong Kong contacts:

Traveller Services (for booking China itineraries)
Room 1012, Silvercord Tower 1
30 Canton Road
Tel: 375 2222; Fax 375 2233

Ministry of Foreign Affairs of the PRC (for
    China visas)
5th Floor, Low Block, China Resources Building
26 Harbour Road, Wanchai
Tel: 585 1794; 585 1700

Dragonair (air service to China)
Room 1843, Swire House
9 Connaught Road, Central District
Tel: 736 0202

CAAC (air service to China)
17 Queen's Road, Central District
    (ground floor)
Tel: 840 1199

A Traveler's Library for China

As a portable but comprehensive guide to the
monuments and civilization of China, nothing
surpasses *Nagle's Encyclopedia-Guide* (Nagle Publishers: Geneva, 1979). *Nagle's* lacks, however,
the updated tips for helping the individual traveler get around that are best provided by *China:
A Travel Survival Kit* (Lonely Planet Publications:
Hawthorn, Victoria, Australia). *Fingertip Chinese*
is, of course the best phrasebook; I say this not
because I wrote it (and hope you just bought it!)
but because the others, especially the popular titles
of Berlitz and Barron's, have yet to be updated. A
rule of thumb for China guides: Don't buy any
that mention using FEC (Foreign Exchange Certificates), which were abandoned in 1994. Another
good language resource is the *Concise English-*

Chinese, Chinese-English Dictionary (Oxford University Press, 1986). Look for the less expensive edition published by the Commercial Press, Hong Kong; it is about the size of *Fingertip Chinese,* only fatter. Even if you are not studying Chinese, it will help when communication problems are encountered. If eating well is a high priority, consult *China's Food* by Nina Simonds, a reasonable compilation of China's better restaurants. It is bulky; photocopy the pages for the places you will be visiting. *The Search for Modern China,* by Jonathan Spence, is the best book on modern Chinese history, replacing John King Fairbank's classic *The United States and China* in this capacity.

List of Lists

Lists of common items and important expressions appear throughout the book under the tasks for which they would obviously be useful. Their locations are also noted in other places where they would be useful to "customize" the sentences introduced. Turning to the list of adjectives on p. 94, for example, would enable you to modify the sentence below to state: "This book is very expensive."

This book is **great**. ("What You Think," p. 94)
*Zhèběn shū **hén hǎo***.
这本书很好.

The "weathermark" identifies this book as a production of Weatherhill, Inc., publishers of fine books on Asia and the Pacific. Book and cover design: Liz Trovato. Production supervision: Bill Rose. Typesetting: Birdtrack Press. Printing and binding: Daamen, Inc., West Rutland, Vermont. English text is set in Adobe Garamond; Chinese is set in *Huákāng Lìjiǎn Sòng*.